PRAXIS 5403 School Psychologist

Rose I. Adams

This page is intentionally left blank.

This publication is not endorsed by any third-party organization. Names of exams are trademarks of respected organizations.

High Learning Group

The text of this publication, or any part thereof, may not be reproduced in any manner whatsoever without written permission from High Learning Group.

Printed in the United States of America

The authors, compilers, and publisher make no warranties regarding the correctness or completeness of the content contained in this publication and specifically disclaim all warranties whatsoever. Advice, strategies, and suggestions described may not be suitable for every case. Providing web addresses or other (information) services in this publication does not mean/imply that the author or publisher endorses information or websites. Neither the author nor the publisher shall be liable for damages arising herefrom. The author and publisher shall not be held responsible for any damage resulting herefrom from the information provided. There are no guarantees attached to the publication. The content of this publication is best practices, suggestions, common mistakes, and interpretation, and the author and the publisher are not responsible for any information contained in the publication.

Disclaimer: By using this book, you agree to the following: High Learning Group and any individual/company/organization/group involved in the development of this publication specifically disclaims any liability (whether based on contract, tort, strict liability, or otherwise) for any direct, indirect, incidental, consequential, or special damages arising out of or in any way connected with access to the information presented in this publication, even if High Learning Group and any individual/company/organization/group involved in the development of this publication have been advised of the possibility of such damages.

High Learning Group and any individual/company/organization/group involved in the development of this publication are not responsible for the use of this information. Information provided through this publication holds no warranty of accuracy, correctness, or truth. The author, publisher, compilers, and all other parties involved in this work disclaim all responsibility for any errors contained within this work and from the results of the use of this information.

No individual or institution has permission to reproduce (in any form) the contents of this publication.

No individual or institution has permission to reproduce the contents on any website.

This page is intentionally left blank.

Table of Content

Chapter 1 – Questions 1

Chapter 2 – Answers and Explanations 58

This page is intentionally left blank.

Chapter 1 – Questions

QUESTION 1

Your school is implementing a mental health awareness program. What is a key component of promoting mental health among students?

- A. Avoiding discussions about mental health to prevent stigma
- B. Providing access to trained mental health professionals for all students
- C. Focusing exclusively on academic achievement without considering mental health
- D. Educating students, staff, and parents about mental health and available resources

Answer:

QUESTION 2

You are tasked with designing an intervention plan for a student who is struggling with reading comprehension. What is the first step you should take to inform your intervention design?

- A. Implement a reading comprehension program without initial assessment
- B. Begin the intervention with standardized tests to track progress
- C. Conduct a comprehensive assessment of the student's reading comprehension skills
- D. Request recommendations from the student's teacher without assessment

Answer:

QUESTION 3

You are evaluating the efficacy of a behavior intervention program for a student with attention difficulties. What is a critical aspect of this evaluation?

- A. Assessing only at the beginning and end of the intervention
- B. Collecting data regularly throughout the intervention
- C. Relying solely on anecdotal reports from the teacher
- D. Discontinuing the intervention after the first assessment

Answer:

QUESTION 4

Your school is implementing a technology-based system to monitor the progress of students receiving individualized education plans (IEPs). What is a key advantage of using technology for progress monitoring?

- A. It reduces the need for individualized assessments
- B. It allows for real-time data collection and analysis
- C. It replaces the need for IEPs altogether
- D. It isolates student progress from other data sources

Answer:

QUESTION 5

You are responsible for evaluating the outcomes of a schoolwide anti-bullying program. What should be the primary focus of your evaluation?

- A. Gathering anecdotal reports from a few teachers
- B. Examining changes in bullying rates and behaviors over time
- C. Ignoring data and relying on general impressions
- D. Conducting a one-time assessment of program effectiveness

Answer:

QUESTION 6

Your school is considering the adoption of a data-driven decision-making system to enhance accountability. What is a crucial aspect to consider when implementing such a system?

   A. Reducing the frequency of data collection to save time
   B. Involving only a select group of staff in decision-making
   C. Ensuring data accuracy and reliability
   D. Ignoring data and relying on intuition

Answer:

QUESTION 7

You are responsible for assessing the impact of a technology-based math intervention program on a group of students. What is a critical step in this assessment process?

   A. Conducting a one-time assessment at the end of the program
   B. Collecting baseline data before the intervention begins
   C. Relying solely on teacher opinions about the program
   D. Disregarding student progress data

Answer:

QUESTION 8

You are working with a student from a culturally diverse family background. The student's family has expressed concerns about their child's academic progress. What is the first step you should take to involve the family effectively in the education process?

   A. Assume the family's concerns are cultural differences and disregard them
   B. Schedule a meeting with the family to discuss their concerns and perspectives
   C. Ignore the family's concerns as they may not align with educational goals
   D. Change the student's curriculum without consulting the family

Answer:

QUESTION 9

Your school is planning a family engagement event. What is a key principle to consider when organizing such an event?

   A. Limit the involvement to a select group of families
   B. Focus solely on academic topics during the event
   C. Ensure that the event is culturally sensitive and inclusive
   D. Exclude educators and school staff from attending

Answer:

QUESTION 10

You are working with a student who is struggling academically, and the student's family has limited English proficiency. What is an effective strategy to involve the family in supporting their child's education?

   A. Avoid involving the family due to language barriers
   B. Provide translated materials and offer interpreters during meetings
   C. Assume the family's lack of English proficiency means they are disinterested
   D. Communicate only through written notes without verbal interaction

Answer:

QUESTION 11

Your school is implementing a family involvement program. What is a critical aspect to consider when promoting collaboration between families and educators?

- A. Limiting the involvement of families to school events only
- B. Encouraging open communication and active listening
- C. Excluding families from decision-making processes
- D. Avoiding collaboration with families from diverse backgrounds

Answer:

QUESTION 12

You are working with a student who has behavioral challenges, and their family is hesitant to participate in the intervention process. What is a recommended strategy to encourage family involvement?

- A. Assume the family is not interested in the intervention process
- B. Provide information about the importance of family involvement and its benefits
- C. Exclude the family from intervention meetings
- D. Implement interventions without family input

Answer:

QUESTION 13

Your school is planning a workshop on effective family-school partnerships. What should be a key focus of this workshop?

- A. Excluding families from the workshop to maintain professionalism
- B. Emphasizing that the school knows best and doesn't need family input
- C. Highlighting the benefits of collaborative relationships between families and educators
- D. Avoiding discussions about the impact of family involvement on student success

Answer:

QUESTION 14

You are working with a student who has a disability, and their parents are concerned about their access to educational services. Which federal law guarantees equal educational opportunities for this student?

- A. Americans with Disabilities Act (ADA)
- B. Elementary and Secondary Education Act (ESEA)
- C. Individuals with Disabilities Education Improvement Act (IDEIA)
- D. Section 504 of the Rehabilitation Act

Answer:

QUESTION 15

A student with a disability is experiencing discrimination in a public school. Which federal law should you refer to when advocating for the student's rights in this situation?

- A. Section 504 of the Rehabilitation Act
- B. Elementary and Secondary Education Act (ESEA)
- C. Americans with Disabilities Act (ADA)
- D. No federal law applies in this case

Answer:

QUESTION 16

A student with a disability has an Individualized Education Program (IEP) in place. However, the school is not adequately implementing the IEP, leading to academic struggles. Which federal law provides legal mechanisms for enforcing the IEP and ensuring appropriate services?

- A. Section 504 of the Rehabilitation Act
- B. Elementary and Secondary Education Act (ESEA)
- C. Individuals with Disabilities Education Improvement Act (IDEIA)
- D. Americans with Disabilities Act (ADA)

Answer:

QUESTION 17

Emma, a 14-year-old student, has been referred for a special education evaluation due to concerns about her academic performance and emotional well-being. After conducting assessments, you find that Emma exhibits significant deficits in reading and mathematics, placing her significantly below her grade level. She also displays symptoms of anxiety and low self-esteem. Based on the assessment data, what is the most appropriate recommendation regarding Emma's eligibility for services?

- A. Emma does not meet the eligibility criteria for special education services.
- B. Emma should receive special education services for her academic deficits only.
- C. Emma should receive special education services for both academic and emotional needs.
- D. Emma should be referred to a general education counselor for emotional support.

Answer:

QUESTION 18

Tyler, a 10-year-old student, has undergone a comprehensive assessment that reveals significant difficulties in reading fluency and comprehension. His assessment data also indicates that he struggles with organization and time management skills, often leading to incomplete assignments. However, Tyler's cognitive abilities are within the average range. What is the most appropriate eligibility recommendation based on this assessment data?

- A. Tyler meets the eligibility criteria for special education services due to his reading difficulties.
- B. Tyler does not meet the eligibility criteria for special education services.
- C. Tyler should receive support for organization and time management but not special education services.
- D. Tyler should be referred to a general education counselor for behavior support.

Answer:

QUESTION 19

After conducting a series of assessments, you determine that a 6-year-old student, Ethan, has a severe speech and language impairment that significantly impacts his communication skills. What is the most appropriate eligibility recommendation based on this assessment data?

- A. Ethan should receive special education services for his speech and language impairment.
- B. Ethan does not meet the eligibility criteria for special education services.
- C. Ethan should receive speech therapy services but not special education services.
- D. Ethan should be referred to a general education counselor for communication support.

Answer:

QUESTION 20

Emily, a 5-year-old child, has recently been diagnosed with a developmental delay. Her parents are concerned about her progress and have requested an Individualized Family Service Plan (IFSP) meeting. You, as a school psychologist, are involved in the development of Emily's IFSP. What is the primary focus of an IFSP for a child like Emily?

- A. The IFSP outlines Emily's special education services and supports.
- B. The IFSP addresses Emily's needs and goals in early childhood intervention.
- C. The IFSP primarily focuses on Emily's academic achievement.
- D. The IFSP discusses Emily's eligibility for special education services.

Answer:

QUESTION 21

When developing an Individualized Education Program (IEP) for a student with a disability, which component is specifically designed to address the student's educational needs and goals?

- A. The annual goals and objectives
- B. The recommended instructional setting
- C. The related services
- D. The testing modifications or accommodations

Answer:

QUESTION 22

John, a 14-year-old student with a learning disability, is in the process of developing his Individualized Education Program (IEP). After conducting assessments, it is clear that John struggles with reading comprehension and written expression. As a school psychologist, which component of John's IEP should be carefully considered to address his specific needs?

- A. The instructional setting or placement
- B. The related services
- C. The annual goals and objectives
- D. The testing modifications or accommodations

Answer:

QUESTION 23

Which component of an Individualized Education Program (IEP) typically outlines the specific services and support that a student with a disability will receive to help them achieve their educational goals?

- A. The annual goals and objectives
- B. The instructional setting or placement
- C. The related services
- D. The testing modifications or accommodations

Answer:

QUESTION 24

Sarah, a 9-year-old student with autism spectrum disorder (ASD), is in the process of developing her Individualized Education Program (IEP). Sarah has made significant progress in her social skills and communication over the past year, but she still struggles with sensory sensitivities that can lead to meltdowns in the classroom. As a school psychologist, which component of Sarah's IEP should be given particular attention to address her sensory sensitivities effectively?

A. The annual goals and objectives
B. The recommended instructional setting or placement
C. The related services
D. The testing modifications or accommodations

Answer:

QUESTION 25

Mark, a 16-year-old student with a specific learning disability (SLD), has been working on his Individualized Education Program (IEP) with the support of an IEP team, including the school psychologist. Mark's IEP includes annual goals for improving his reading and writing skills. However, recent progress monitoring data show that Mark has not made significant progress toward these goals. What should the IEP team, including the school psychologist, do to address this situation effectively?

A. Modify the annual goals and objectives to be more challenging.
B. Keep the goals the same but increase the frequency of progress monitoring.
C. Review and revise the instructional strategies and interventions.
D. Discontinue the IEP since it is not leading to significant progress.

Answer:

QUESTION 26

Emily, a 7-year-old student with attention deficit hyperactivity disorder (ADHD), has an Individualized Education Program (IEP) that includes annual goals for improving her attention and self-regulation skills. Emily's progress monitoring data indicate that she is making good progress toward these goals. However, her classroom teacher reports that Emily still struggles to stay focused and organized in class. What should the IEP team, including the school psychologist, consider doing to address this situation?

A. Adjust the annual goals to be more ambitious.
B. Provide additional related services, such as counseling.
C. Ensure better alignment between the IEP goals and classroom strategies.
D. Remove the annual goals since Emily is making progress.

Answer:

QUESTION 27

You are a school psychologist tasked with evaluating the effectiveness of a school's reading intervention program for struggling readers. The program has been in place for two years. You have collected data on student reading scores before and after implementing the program. What statistical procedure should you use to determine the program's effectiveness in improving student reading skills?

A. Chi-squared test
B. Paired-samples t-test
C. Analysis of Variance (ANOVA)
D. Pearson correlation coefficient

Answer:

QUESTION 28

When evaluating the effectiveness of a newly implemented classroom behavior management program, which research design would be most appropriate for assessing the program's impact on student behavior over time?

   A. Case study design
   B. Cross-sectional design
   C. Longitudinal design
   D. Ethnographic design

Answer:

QUESTION 29

You are planning to conduct a program evaluation to assess the effectiveness of a school's counseling services on students' well-being. What research methodology would be most appropriate for gathering in-depth insights into students' experiences and perceptions of the counseling services?

   A. Experimental design
   B. Survey research
   C. Qualitative research
   D. Correlational research

Answer:

QUESTION 30

You are tasked with selecting an assessment instrument to evaluate a school-wide character education program's impact on students' social and emotional development. What should be a primary consideration when choosing the assessment instrument for this program evaluation?

   A. The instrument's popularity among educators
   B. The cost of administering the assessment
   C. The reliability and validity of the assessment instrument
   D. The length of time required to complete the assessment

Answer:

QUESTION 31

You are a school psychologist working with a 10-year-old student, Sarah, who has been experiencing behavioral challenges in the classroom. Sarah's teacher has requested your assistance in addressing these challenges. After conducting assessments, you have identified specific behavioral interventions that may be effective for Sarah. What is the most appropriate next step in the consultation and collaboration process?

   A. Implement the behavioral interventions without consulting others.
   B. Share the assessment findings and proposed interventions with Sarah's teacher and seek their input and collaboration.
   C. Maintain confidentiality and avoid discussing Sarah's challenges with anyone.
   D. Refer Sarah to an external behavior specialist for intervention.

Answer:

QUESTION 32

When collaborating with parents/guardians to address a student's academic difficulties, what is a critical aspect of maintaining effective communication and collaboration?

   A. Sharing only positive information about the student's progress
   B. Providing solutions and recommendations without seeking input
   C. Actively listening to parents' concerns and involving them in the problem-solving process
   D. Keeping assessment results confidential and not sharing them with parents

Answer:

QUESTION 33

You are working with a student, Alex, who has been referred for assessment due to reading difficulties. After conducting assessments, you have identified specific reading interventions that may benefit Alex. In a collaborative meeting with Alex's teacher, the teacher expresses concerns about implementing the interventions due to limited classroom resources. What is the most appropriate course of action in this situation?

- A. Disregard the teacher's concerns and proceed with implementing the interventions as planned.
- B. Collaboratively explore alternative strategies and resources that can support the implementation of the interventions.
- C. Recommend that the teacher seek additional funding for classroom resources independently.
- D. Refer Alex to another school with more resources.

Answer:

QUESTION 34

As a school psychologist, you have been consistently attending professional development workshops and conferences to stay updated with the latest research and practices in the field. During a conference, you come across a new assessment tool that appears to have significant potential for improving your assessments. What should be your next step to ensure effective integration of this tool into your practice?

- A. Immediately start using the new assessment tool with your students.
- B. Share the tool with your colleagues without further investigation.
- C. Conduct thorough research on the tool, including its reliability, validity, and appropriateness for your specific context.
- D. Attend more conferences to find additional assessment tools.

Answer:

QUESTION 35

When considering the importance of continued professional development, which statement best reflects the rationale behind actively engaging in ongoing learning and growth as a school psychologist?

- A. Continued professional development is necessary to maintain employment.
- B. Ongoing learning ensures that school psychologists remain up-to-date with the latest research and best practices.
- C. Professional development is only relevant for new school psychologists.
- D. Once a school psychologist completes their initial training, they do not need further development.

Answer:

QUESTION 36

You are a school psychologist responsible for training and supporting colleagues in your school district on the use of educational technology tools to enhance their assessments and interventions. You have recently discovered a new technology platform that can significantly streamline data collection and analysis. What is the most effective way to share this discovery with your colleagues and encourage its adoption?

- A. Share a brief email about the technology platform's features and benefits.
- B. Conduct a hands-on workshop to demonstrate the platform's functionality and benefits.
- C. Mention the technology platform in passing during a staff meeting.
- D. Keep the discovery to yourself to maintain a competitive edge.

Answer:

QUESTION 37

A high school student has been consistently disruptive in class and appears agitated. The teacher suspects the student may be using drugs. As a School Psychologist, which of the following variables would be most relevant to consider when assessing the situation?

A. Socioeconomic status
B. Parent and teacher expectations
C. Linguistic variables
D. Psychopathological variables

Answer:

QUESTION 38

A kindergarten student is struggling to communicate effectively and exhibits limited language development. Which variable is most likely influencing this child's linguistic development?

A. Socioeconomic status
B. Family issues
C. Biological temperament
D. Chemical use or abuse

Answer:

QUESTION 39

A 10-year-old student from a low-income family frequently arrives at school hungry and is often fatigued in class. What variable should be the primary focus when considering the student's behavior and development?

A. Cultural or ethnic background
B. Prior experiences
C. Prenatal and early environment
D. Socioeconomic status

Answer:

QUESTION 40

You are working with a teenage student who exhibits aggressive behavior towards peers. After assessing the situation, you discover a history of domestic violence in the student's family. Which variable is most likely contributing to the student's aggressive behavior?

A. Gender-related variables
B. Parent and teacher expectations
C. Cultural or ethnic background
D. Family issues

Answer:

QUESTION 41

A 7-year-old student consistently underperforms academically despite having no identified learning disabilities. What variable should you consider to better understand this student's academic challenges?

A. Biological development
B. Social interactions
C. Teacher expectations
D. Cultural or ethnic background

Answer:

QUESTION 42

A middle school student is struggling with emotional regulation and frequently has outbursts in class. After interviewing the student's parents, you learn that they have high expectations for their child to excel academically. Which variable may be contributing to the student's emotional struggles?

- A. Psychopathological variables
- B. Biological development
- C. Gender-related variables
- D. Parent and teacher expectations

Answer:

QUESTION 43

You are working with a student who has attention deficit hyperactivity disorder (ADHD). The student struggles with staying focused in a traditional classroom setting. Which type of learning environment is most likely to benefit this student's needs?

- A. Large, lecture-style classroom
- B. Small, self-paced online courses
- C. Structured, teacher-led classroom
- D. Highly social, group learning environment

Answer:

QUESTION 44

A 10-year-old student with autism spectrum disorder (ASD) has difficulty with social interactions and communication. What learning environment modification should be prioritized to support this student's needs?

- A. Inclusion in a regular classroom with neurotypical peers
- B. One-on-one tutoring sessions
- C. Special education classroom with ASD-specific interventions
- D. Extracurricular group activities

Answer:

QUESTION 45

You are working with a student who has a significant auditory processing disorder. Which learning environment modification is most appropriate for this student?

- A. Visual aids and written instructions
- B. Frequent group discussions
- C. Classroom with background music
- D. Lecture-based instruction

Answer:

QUESTION 46

A 7-year-old student with behavioral challenges often disrupts the class and struggles with impulse control. Which classroom management strategy should be employed to address this student's behavior effectively?

- A. Frequent time-outs in a designated area
- B. Strict discipline and consequences for misbehavior
- C. Positive behavior reinforcement and a token system
- D. Assigning extra homework for disruptive behavior

Answer:

QUESTION 47

You are working with a student who experiences high levels of test anxiety. Which intervention technique is most likely to help this student manage their anxiety and improve their academic performance?

- A. Increasing the frequency of quizzes and tests
- B. Providing relaxation techniques before assessments
- C. Assigning more homework assignments
- D. Isolating the student during assessments

Answer:

QUESTION 48

A 13-year-old student is struggling with low self-esteem and social isolation. Which type of learning environment is most likely to promote this student's social and emotional development?

- A. Strict, rule-focused classroom
- B. Highly competitive academic environment
- C. Collaborative and inclusive classroom
- D. Individualized, self-paced learning

Answer:

QUESTION 49

You are a School Psychologist working with a 9-year-old student named Emma. Emma has been diagnosed with dyslexia, a reading disorder that makes it difficult for her to decode and comprehend written text. She often becomes frustrated during reading activities in her regular classroom, which has led to behavioral issues. Her teacher believes that Emma might benefit from a different learning environment Which modification to Emma's learning environment is most appropriate to support her needs?

- A. Enrolling Emma in a highly competitive academic program
- B. Providing Emma with extra homework assignments to improve her reading skills
- C. Placing Emma in a small group reading intervention class
- D. Increasing the frequency of traditional lecture-style lessons

Answer:

QUESTION 50

You are working with a 14-year-old student named Alex, who has been identified as having attention deficit hyperactivity disorder (ADHD). Alex often disrupts the class with impulsive behavior and struggles to stay focused during lectures. The traditional classroom environment is not conducive to his learning style. Which modification to Alex's learning environment is most likely to benefit him?

- A. Increasing the length of classroom lectures
- B. Assigning more group projects that require collaboration
- C. Providing a quiet and structured workspace with minimal distractions
- D. Enrolling Alex in an advanced academic program

Answer:

QUESTION 51

You are working with a 12-year-old student named Liam, who has social anxiety and struggles with participating in classroom discussions. Liam's anxiety is impacting his academic performance and social interactions with peers. What modification to Liam's learning environment and classroom management strategy is most appropriate to support his needs?

A. Encouraging Liam to lead group discussions to boost his confidence
B. Assigning more frequent written assignments to reduce the need for verbal participation
C. Providing opportunities for peer-assisted learning and group projects
D. Allowing Liam to opt-out of classroom discussions entirely

Answer:

QUESTION 52

A school psychologist is selecting an assessment instrument to evaluate a student's reading abilities. Which psychometric property should the psychologist consider most when deciding on an assessment tool?

A. Test-retest reliability
B. Face validity
C. Convergent validity
D. Content validity

Answer:

QUESTION 53

You are working with a culturally diverse group of students, and you need to select an assessment tool to measure their academic performance. What important consideration should guide your choice of assessment instrument in this context?

A. The availability of normative data for the specific cultural group
B. The length and complexity of the assessment
C. The cost of the assessment tool
D. The alignment of the assessment with state standards

Answer:

QUESTION 54

A school psychologist is evaluating a new intelligence test for potential use in their assessments. The psychologist is concerned about potential bias in the test. Which type of bias should the psychologist be most cautious of when assessing the test's appropriateness?

A. Gender bias
B. Age bias
C. Socioeconomic bias
D. Test-retest bias

Answer:

QUESTION 55

You are conducting an assessment of a preschool child with limited English proficiency. The child's home language is not English. What should be a primary consideration when selecting assessment methods and techniques for this child?

A. Using assessment tools designed for older children to challenge the child's language skills
B. Conducting the assessment solely in English to promote language acquisition
C. Utilizing culturally and linguistically appropriate assessment tools and techniques
D. Skipping the assessment due to the child's limited English proficiency

Answer:

QUESTION 56

A school psychologist is selecting an assessment tool to measure the social-emotional development of elementary school students. Which type of validity should the psychologist prioritize to ensure the assessment accurately measures the intended construct?

- A. Criterion validity
- B. Content validity
- C. Construct validity
- D. Concurrent validity

Answer:

QUESTION 57

You are tasked with assessing a child who has recently experienced a traumatic event. It is essential to establish rapport and a comfortable testing environment. Which ethical principle is most relevant in this situation?

- A. Autonomy
- B. Beneficence
- C. Non-maleficence
- D. Veracity

Answer:

QUESTION 58

A school psychologist is tasked with assessing the academic progress of a culturally diverse group of students, including English language learners (ELLs). Which assessment strategy is most appropriate to ensure nondiscriminatory assessment for this group?

- A. Administering the assessment only in English to maintain consistency
- B. Providing accommodations, such as bilingual dictionaries, for ELLs during the assessment
- C. Excluding ELLs from the assessment to prevent potential bias
- D. Using a standardized assessment with no consideration for cultural diversity

Answer:

QUESTION 59

You are conducting an assessment of a student with a hearing impairment. The student primarily communicates through sign language. Which approach should you consider when administering assessments to this student to ensure accurate and useful information for planning instruction?

- A. Administering written assessments to evaluate language proficiency
- B. Providing oral instructions and relying on lip reading
- C. Using sign language interpreters and providing assessments in sign language
- D. Excluding the student from assessments due to communication challenges

Answer:

QUESTION 60

A school psychologist is assessing a student with limited English proficiency for a special education program. The psychologist recognizes the significance of linguistic diversity. What should be the psychologist's primary consideration when administering assessments in this case?

- A. Administering assessments only in English to maintain consistency
- B. Providing additional time for English language learners (ELLs) to complete assessments
- C. Using assessments in the student's native language, if available and appropriate
- D. Excluding ELLs from assessments to avoid potential bias

Answer:

QUESTION 61

You are working with a student who has a severe visual impairment and requires specialized assessment methods. Which assessment approach is most appropriate to provide accurate and useful information for planning instruction and modifications?

A. Administering traditional written assessments with accommodations
B. Providing oral assessments to the student
C. Using tactile or Braille-based assessments as needed
D. Exempting the student from assessments due to the visual impairment

Answer:

QUESTION 62

A school psychologist is assessing a culturally diverse group of students. What should the psychologist consider to ensure the assessments are nondiscriminatory and provide useful information for instructional planning?

A. Administering assessments uniformly to all students without accommodations
B. Providing culturally biased assessments to maintain consistency
C. Using assessment measures that consider linguistic and cultural diversity
D. Excluding students from assessments if they come from diverse backgrounds

Answer:

QUESTION 63

You are tasked with assessing a group of students who come from low socioeconomic backgrounds. Many of these students face economic challenges in their daily lives. What should be your primary consideration when administering assessments to this group?

A. Providing financial incentives to motivate students during assessments
B. Ensuring that assessments are culturally biased to match students' socioeconomic backgrounds
C. Offering a supportive and empathetic testing environment
D. Excluding students from assessments due to socioeconomic challenges

Answer:

QUESTION 64

You are a school psychologist tasked with assessing a group of culturally diverse students, including recent immigrants. Many of these students have limited English proficiency. As you plan the assessments, you notice that the standardized assessments available are primarily in English. What should you do to ensure fair and accurate assessment for these students?

A. Administer the assessments in English, as it provides a consistent standard.
B. Utilize interpreters and translated assessments in the students' native languages.
C. Exclude students with limited English proficiency from the assessments.
D. Use non-standardized, informal assessments to avoid language barriers.

Answer:

QUESTION 65

You are working with a student who has a physical disability that affects their motor skills. The standardized assessments typically used are not accessible to this student. The student's disability does not affect their cognitive abilities. What should be your primary consideration when planning assessments for this student?

A. Administer the same standardized assessments used for other students, even if they are not accessible.
B. Request an exemption from assessments for the student due to their physical disability.
C. Select or adapt assessments that are accessible and measure the student's cognitive abilities accurately.
D. Provide additional time for the student to complete the assessments, considering their motor difficulties.

Answer:

QUESTION 66

You are conducting assessments for a group of students from low socioeconomic backgrounds. Many of these students face financial challenges and may not have access to educational resources at home. You want to ensure that the assessments are fair and considerate of their circumstances. What approach should you take to provide equitable assessments for these students?

A. Offer financial incentives to motivate students during assessments.
B. Use assessments that require expensive materials or technology to challenge students.
C. Modify the assessments to be more difficult for these students to promote resilience.
D. Provide a supportive and understanding testing environment that considers their economic challenges.

Answer:

QUESTION 67

A school psychologist reviews a student's assessment data, which includes cognitive and academic assessments. The data show that the student scored below average on a reading assessment. What conclusion can be drawn from this assessment data?

A. The student has a specific learning disability in reading.
B. The student will excel in all academic subjects except reading.
C. The student will never catch up to their peers in reading skills.
D. The student's reading difficulties are solely due to a lack of effort.

Answer:

QUESTION 68

You are reviewing the assessment data of a 15-year-old student. The data indicate that the student has consistently performed well on cognitive assessments but struggles with emotional regulation and social interactions. What conclusion can be drawn from this assessment data?

A. The student has a high IQ and does not require support for emotional and social difficulties.
B. The student may have an emotional or social disorder that requires attention.
C. The student's emotional and social difficulties are a result of a low IQ.
D. The student's emotional and social struggles are temporary and will resolve on their own.

Answer:

QUESTION 69

A school psychologist reviews a student's assessment data, which includes measures of attention and hyperactivity. The data show that the student exhibits significant attention difficulties and hyperactivity. What conclusion can be drawn from this assessment data?

A. The student is likely to outgrow these attention difficulties and hyperactivity.
B. The student may have attention deficit hyperactivity disorder (ADHD) or a similar condition.
C. The student's difficulties are solely the result of inadequate classroom instruction.
D. The student's attention and hyperactivity issues are unrelated to their academic performance.

Answer:

QUESTION 70

You are examining assessment data for a 12-year-old student. The data reveal that the student consistently scores well on academic assessments but exhibits extreme anxiety in test-taking situations. What conclusion can be drawn from this assessment data?

A. The student's anxiety is unrelated to their academic performance.
B. The student is not truly anxious and is using it as an excuse for poor performance.
C. The student may have test anxiety that impacts their performance.
D. The student has no need for academic support or accommodations.

Answer:

QUESTION 71

A school psychologist reviews a student's assessment data, which includes measures of behavior and social interactions. The data indicate that the student exhibits aggressive behavior towards peers but is well-behaved at home. What conclusion can be drawn from this assessment data?

A. The student has a conduct disorder that requires residential treatment.
B. The student's aggressive behavior is consistent across all settings.
C. The student's aggressive behavior is limited to the school environment.
D. The student's behavior is entirely due to the influence of their peers.

Answer:

QUESTION 72

You are examining assessment data for a 7-year-old student with inconsistent academic performance. The data show that the student excels in some subjects but struggles significantly in others. What conclusion can be drawn from this assessment data?

A. The student's inconsistent performance is indicative of a lack of effort.
B. The student has a learning disability that affects specific subjects.
C. The student is not suited for traditional academic instruction.
D. The student's inconsistent performance is a result of poor teaching.

Answer:

QUESTION 73

You are working with a 10-year-old student who exhibits disruptive behavior in the classroom. After conducting a functional-behavioral assessment, you identify that the student's disruptive behavior typically occurs when they are asked to complete challenging math tasks. What is the most appropriate step to take based on this assessment information?

A. Exclude the student from math instruction to prevent disruptive behavior.
B. Develop a behavior intervention plan (BIP) that includes strategies to address the student's challenging math tasks.
C. Increase the academic demands on the student to build resilience.
D. Place the student in a separate special education classroom.

Answer:

QUESTION 74

A school psychologist is working with a student who has been identified as needing special education services. The student's individualized education program (IEP) team is considering placement options. What should be the primary consideration when determining the appropriate placement within the continuum of the least restrictive environment?

A. The availability of space in special education classrooms
B. The convenience of transportation for the student
C. The student's unique learning needs and the potential for inclusion in general education settings
D. The cost-effectiveness of placement options

Answer:

QUESTION 75

You are part of an IEP team for a student with autism spectrum disorder (ASD). The team is discussing placement options. The student has shown significant progress in communication skills but struggles with social interactions. What placement option should be considered to provide the least restrictive environment?

- A. Placement in a separate special education classroom for students with ASD
- B. Placement in a general education classroom with additional support and accommodations
- C. Placement in a residential treatment facility
- D. Placement in a self-contained classroom for students with behavioral disorders

Answer:

QUESTION 76

A school psychologist is conducting a functional-behavioral assessment for a student who exhibits aggressive behavior in the classroom. The assessment reveals that the student's aggression often occurs when they are asked to complete written assignments. What is the next step in the process of developing appropriate behavior intervention plans (BIPs)?

- A. Recommending immediate expulsion from school to protect other students
- B. Identifying appropriate alternative behaviors to replace the aggression
- C. Increasing the frequency of written assignments to desensitize the student
- D. Placing the student in a segregated special education classroom

Answer:

QUESTION 77

This question is intentionally removed.

QUESTION 78

This question is intentionally removed.

QUESTION 79

This question is intentionally removed.

QUESTION 80

You are working with a student named Maria, who has a significant intellectual disability and requires assistance with daily living skills, including feeding and toileting. Maria's IEP team is considering placement options for her education. Maria's assessment data indicate that her cognitive abilities are severely limited, and she requires constant support for all aspects of her daily life. What placement option should the IEP team prioritize to provide Maria with the least restrictive environment while addressing her needs?

- A. Placement in a general education classroom with extensive paraprofessional support
- B. Placement in a separate special education classroom for students with severe intellectual disabilities
- C. Placement in a residential treatment facility to provide comprehensive care
- D. Placement in a self-contained classroom for students with multiple disabilities

Answer:

QUESTION 81

A school psychologist is tasked with presenting research findings on effective interventions for improving reading comprehension to a group of teachers and parents. Which strategy would be most effective in ensuring that the information is accessible and understandable to the audience?

A. Presenting complex statistical data and research methodologies to demonstrate expertise
B. Using plain language and real-life examples to explain the interventions and their impact
C. Omitting specific research findings to avoid overwhelming the audience
D. Providing only written materials without a verbal presentation

Answer:

QUESTION 82

A school psychologist is conducting a study to evaluate the outcomes of a new reading intervention program implemented in a school district. What is a critical aspect of data-based decision making in this research context?

A. Reporting only the positive outcomes of the intervention to maintain a positive image of the program
B. Utilizing a single data point to draw conclusions about the program's effectiveness
C. Using multiple sources of data, such as pre- and post-assessments and teacher observations
D. Ignoring the feedback from teachers and students involved in the program

Answer:

QUESTION 83

You are conducting research to identify factors that influence student motivation in a specific school district. After analyzing the data, you find that a lack of access to extracurricular activities is negatively impacting student motivation. How should you approach the dissemination of these research findings to the district's administrators?

A. Keeping the findings confidential to avoid potential controversy
B. Focusing solely on the academic factors influencing motivation
C. Providing a comprehensive report that includes recommendations for increasing access to extracurricular activities
D. Omitting any recommendations and leaving it to the administrators to interpret the findings

Answer:

QUESTION 84

A school psychologist is tasked with presenting research findings on the impact of classroom size on student achievement to parents and the public. What communication strategy would be most effective in this situation?

A. Using technical jargon and complex statistical analyses to demonstrate expertise
B. Creating colorful and visually appealing charts without detailed explanations
C. Preparing a clear and concise presentation that highlights key findings and their implications
D. Sharing the research findings only with a select group of parents to maintain control over the information

Answer:

QUESTION 85

A school psychologist is working with a diverse group of teachers and parents during a consultation meeting to address a student's behavioral challenges. The meeting becomes contentious, with participants expressing conflicting viewpoints. What interpersonal skill is most important for the psychologist to employ in this situation?

A. Providing immediate solutions to end the conflict
B. Demonstrating active listening and empathy
C. Avoiding the discussion of cultural diversity to prevent further conflict
D. Taking a dominant role in the meeting to maintain control

Answer:

QUESTION 86

You are a school psychologist working with a group of teachers from different cultural backgrounds who are experiencing conflict within their team. The conflict arises from differences in teaching approaches and communication styles. How should you approach facilitating a resolution to this conflict while considering cultural diversity?

A. Encourage the teachers to conform to a single, culturally neutral teaching approach
B. Avoid addressing cultural differences to prevent further tension
C. Facilitate open and respectful discussions about cultural diversity and its impact on teaching practices
D. Suggest that the teachers work individually without collaborating to avoid conflict

Answer:

QUESTION 87

A school psychologist is conducting a consultation session with a group of parents from various cultural backgrounds. The parents have expressed concerns about the school's approach to discipline, which they feel is inconsistent and culturally insensitive. What is the psychologist's most appropriate course of action?

A. Disregard the parents' concerns as individual perspectives and maintain the current disciplinary practices
B. Acknowledge the parents' concerns and work collaboratively to develop a discipline policy that respects cultural diversity
C. Recommend that the parents adapt to the school's disciplinary approach to maintain consistency
D. Exclude the parents from discussions on disciplinary matters to prevent further conflicts

Answer:

QUESTION 88

You are facilitating a consultation meeting with a diverse group of educators to discuss strategies for improving student engagement in a culturally diverse classroom. During the meeting, participants express different viewpoints on effective strategies. Some educators suggest that incorporating culturally relevant materials is essential, while others believe that focusing solely on the curriculum is sufficient. What is the psychologist's role in this consultation process?

A. Taking a dominant role and imposing a single approach that aligns with the psychologist's perspective
B. Facilitating open and respectful discussions that allow educators to explore different strategies and reach a consensus
C. Ignoring the cultural diversity aspect and focusing solely on curriculum-based strategies
D. Excluding educators with opposing viewpoints to maintain a cohesive approach

Answer:

QUESTION 89

A school psychologist is consulting with a group of teachers who are experiencing conflicts in their interactions with parents from culturally diverse backgrounds. The teachers express frustration and feel ill-equipped to address the issues. What interpersonal skill should the psychologist emphasize to help the teachers navigate these challenges effectively?

A. Encouraging the teachers to assertively confront parents about their concerns
B. Teaching the teachers to avoid discussing cultural diversity to prevent conflicts
C. Providing conflict resolution strategies that consider cultural sensitivity and empathy
D. Advising the teachers to maintain a dominant stance in interactions with parents

Answer:

QUESTION 90

A school psychologist is working with a student who has recently experienced a traumatic event. The psychologist must provide counseling services as part of their role. How does the historical foundation of psychology influence the school psychologist's approach to trauma counseling?

 A. The historical foundation suggests that trauma should be minimized and avoided to maintain psychological well-being.
 B. The historical foundation emphasizes the importance of acknowledging and addressing trauma as a critical aspect of psychological well-being.
 C. The historical foundation encourages school psychologists to avoid discussing trauma with students to prevent further distress.
 D. The historical foundation promotes the idea that trauma is irrelevant to psychological health.

Answer

QUESTION 91

You are a school psychologist in a district that has recently implemented a new policy regarding mandated reporting of child abuse and neglect. The policy requires all school personnel, including psychologists, to report any suspected cases of abuse or neglect promptly. However, you become aware of a situation where a student might be at risk, but you are uncertain about the facts. What ethical principle should guide your decision on whether to report the situation, considering the legal requirements and standards of professional practice?

 A. Maintain confidentiality at all costs to protect the student's privacy.
 B. Report the situation immediately based on the suspicion, as it aligns with the legal mandate.
 C. Gather more information to confirm the suspicion before making a report.
 D. Avoid reporting the situation to prevent potential harm to the student's family.

Answer:

QUESTION 92

A school psychologist is conducting an assessment of a student's cognitive abilities. The psychologist wants to ensure that the assessment aligns with ethical standards and legal requirements. What should the psychologist consider during the assessment process?

 A. Providing the student with the answers to build self-esteem
 B. Administering the assessment without obtaining informed consent from the student's parents
 C. Ensuring that the assessment is valid and culturally sensitive
 D. Withholding the assessment results to prevent potential harm to the student

Answer:

QUESTION 93

You are a school psychologist working with a student who has disclosed experiencing bullying by a classmate. The student is afraid and unsure of what to do. What should be your primary ethical and professional responsibility in this situation?

 A. Disregard the student's disclosure to avoid potential conflicts with the school administration.
 B. Provide immediate support to the student and report the bullying incident according to legal and ethical requirements.
 C. Encourage the student to confront the bully independently to build resilience.
 D. Advise the student to keep the bullying incident a secret to avoid further harm.

Answer:

QUESTION 94

A school psychologist is asked to provide counseling services to a student who has disclosed suicidal thoughts. The psychologist is concerned about the student's safety. What is the appropriate ethical and legal course of action in this situation?

- A. Keep the student's disclosure confidential to respect their privacy.
- B. Notify the student's parents without the student's consent to ensure immediate support.
- C. Advise the student to handle the situation independently to build resilience.
- D. Consult with school administrators but avoid any intervention without the student's permission.

Answer:

QUESTION 95

In a school setting, a student with Attention-Deficit/Hyperactivity Disorder (ADHD) has been prescribed medication to manage their symptoms. What is the primary reason for using medication in this case?

- A. To cure ADHD
- B. To enhance cognitive abilities
- C. To alleviate symptoms and improve focus
- D. To boost social skills

Answer:

QUESTION 96

A 10-year-old gifted student is displaying signs of underachievement in the classroom. What should a school psychologist consider when assessing this situation?

- A. Accelerating the student to a higher grade level
- B. Providing enrichment activities
- C. Suspecting a learning disability
- D. Recommending medication for the student

Answer:

QUESTION 97

A 7-year-old student with a specific learning disability in reading is receiving special education services. What medication is most commonly used to treat reading disorders like dyslexia?

- A. Ritalin
- B. Adderall
- C. None, medication is not a standard treatment for dyslexia
- D. Antidepressants

Answer:

QUESTION 98

A high school student is struggling with anxiety and has been prescribed medication by a physician. As a school psychologist, what is your role in this situation?

- A. Determine the medication dosage
- B. Monitor the student's medication compliance
- C. Provide therapy to replace medication
- D. Encourage the student to stop taking the medication

Answer:

QUESTION 99

A student with autism spectrum disorder (ASD) is experiencing sensory sensitivities that interfere with their classroom participation. What is a non-pharmacological intervention that may be beneficial in this case?

A. Prescribing an anti-anxiety medication
B. Conducting a neuropsychological assessment
C. Providing sensory accommodations like noise-canceling headphones
D. Recommending cognitive-behavioral therapy

Answer:

QUESTION 100

A preschool-age child has been identified as gifted in the domain of language development. What is a common characteristic of giftedness in this domain?

A. Delayed speech and language milestones
B. Difficulty in forming social relationships
C. Advanced vocabulary and early reading skills
D. A preference for sensorimotor activities

Answer:

QUESTION 101

A student with autism spectrum disorder (ASD) struggles with sensory sensitivities and frequent meltdowns in the classroom. What is the most effective strategy for modifying the learning environment to support this student?

A. Reducing sensory stimulation to a minimum
B. Completely eliminating sensory stimuli
C. Providing a variety of sensory experiences
D. Ignoring the sensory sensitivities

Answer:

QUESTION 102

A middle school student with attention difficulties consistently fails to complete homework assignments. What modification to the learning environment can best address this issue?

A. Assigning more homework to improve focus
B. Providing a quiet and organized homework space
C. Reducing all assignments to shorter tasks
D. Implementing stricter consequences for incomplete homework

Answer:

QUESTION 103

A child with a specific learning disability in reading has difficulty decoding words. What modification to the learning environment is most appropriate for this student?

A. Providing extra time for math assignments
B. Offering audiobooks and text-to-speech software
C. Assigning more complex reading materials
D. Increasing the reading speed expectations

Answer:

QUESTION 104

You are working with a student with emotional and behavioral challenges who frequently exhibits aggressive behavior towards peers. What is a proactive strategy for modifying the learning environment to reduce these behaviors?

- A. Implementing a zero-tolerance policy for aggression
- B. Providing clear behavior expectations and positive reinforcement
- C. Isolating the student from their peers during breaks
- D. Punishing the student for aggressive behavior

Answer:

QUESTION 105

You are assisting parents in implementing a behavior-change program at home for a child with autism. What is a key principle of generalization that should be emphasized to the parents?

- A. Keep the intervention entirely separate from the school environment
- B. Implement the intervention in only one setting to avoid confusion
- C. Ensure that the intervention strategies are used consistently across different settings
- D. Avoid discussing the intervention with other caregivers or teachers

Answer:

QUESTION 106

A high school student is transitioning from a special education program to a mainstream classroom. What is a crucial consideration in facilitating this transition?

- A. Delaying the transition until the student is fully prepared
- B. Maintaining separate curricula for special education and mainstream settings
- C. Providing appropriate support and accommodations in the mainstream classroom
- D. Avoiding any communication with the student's parents about the transition

Answer:

QUESTION 107

Sarah is a 5th-grade student with Attention-Deficit/Hyperactivity Disorder (ADHD). She often struggles to stay focused in the classroom and frequently forgets to complete her assignments. Despite receiving medication and some classroom accommodations, Sarah's academic performance remains inconsistent. Which modification to the learning environment would be most beneficial for Sarah in this case?

- A. Assigning additional homework to improve her concentration
- B. Providing her with a quiet and organized workspace
- C. Reducing all assignments to shorter tasks
- D. Implementing stricter consequences for incomplete assignments

Answer:

QUESTION 108

Ethan is a 7th-grade student with autism spectrum disorder (ASD) who has made significant progress in improving his social communication skills through therapy. His parents and teachers have noticed that he interacts well with peers and adults in structured settings, such as the therapy clinic. However, his social communication skills do not seem to generalize to less structured environments like the school cafeteria and playground. What is a key principle that should guide interventions to help Ethan generalize his social communication skills effectively?

A. Limit his social interactions to structured settings only
B. Provide fewer opportunities for social interaction in unstructured environments
C. Encourage practice and support in various unstructured social settings
D. Remove him from unstructured settings to avoid frustration

Answer:

QUESTION 109

Olivia is a high school student with a specific learning disability in mathematics. She has been receiving individualized instruction and support in a resource room to improve her math skills. Olivia's parents are concerned about her ability to apply what she's learned in the resource room to her regular math class, where the environment is different and more challenging. What would be a recommended strategy to facilitate the transfer of Olivia's math skills from the resource room to her regular math class?

A. Ensure Olivia's regular math class uses a different curriculum than the resource room
B. Encourage Olivia to rely solely on the resource room for math instruction
C. Promote collaboration between the resource room teacher and the regular math teacher
D. Isolate Olivia from her regular math class to minimize distractions

Answer:

QUESTION 110

You are reviewing the test results of a student who recently underwent a cognitive assessment. The student's Full-Scale IQ score is 85. What does this score indicate?

A. The student's cognitive abilities are above average
B. The student's cognitive abilities are below average
C. The student's cognitive abilities are average
D. The student's cognitive abilities cannot be determined from this score

Answer:

QUESTION 111

You are analyzing the results of a standardized reading assessment for a group of 5th-grade students. The mean score for the group is 75, and the standard deviation is 10. If a student scored 85 on the assessment, what can you conclude about their performance?

A. The student's score is above average
B. The student's score is below average
C. The student's score is exactly average
D. The student's score is not interpretable based on the information provided

Answer:

QUESTION 112

You are interpreting the results of a standardized test for a 10-year-old student. The student's score places them at the 75th percentile. What does this mean?

A. The student scored higher than 75% of students in the norming group
B. The student scored lower than 75% of students in the norming group
C. The student scored exactly at the median of the norming group
D. The student's score is not interpretable based on the percentile rank

Answer:

QUESTION 113

You are conducting an assessment of a child's academic abilities. The child's grade-equivalent score for reading is 4.5. What does this score signify?

A. The child is reading at a 4th-grade level
B. The child is reading at a 5th-grade level
C. The child is reading at an average level for their age
D. The child's reading abilities cannot be determined from this score

Answer:

QUESTION 114

You are reviewing a student's test results, and you notice that their z-score for a particular assessment is -1.5. What does this z-score tell you about the student's performance?

A. The student's performance is 1.5 standard deviations above the mean
B. The student's performance is 1.5 standard deviations below the mean
C. The student's performance is exactly at the mean
D. The student's performance is not interpretable based on the z-score

Answer:

QUESTION 115

You are analyzing the test results of a group of students who completed a mathematics assessment. The standard deviation of their scores is 5. If a student's score is 10, what can you conclude about their performance?

A. The student's score is above average
B. The student's score is below average
C. The student's score is exactly average
D. The student's score is not interpretable based on the information provided

Answer:

QUESTION 116

You have conducted a comprehensive assessment of a 9-year-old student with learning difficulties. The assessment results indicate a significant deficit in phonological processing skills. The parents request an explanation of what this means for their child's learning. How should you communicate this assessment result to the parents?

A. Provide a detailed explanation of phonological processing without using jargon
B. Direct the parents to research phonological processing on their own
C. Tell the parents it is a common issue that will likely resolve on its own
D. Avoid discussing the assessment results with the parents

Answer:

QUESTION 117

You are writing an assessment report for a 7-year-old student with attention difficulties. What should be the primary focus when preparing the report?

- A. Providing minimal information to keep the report concise
- B. Using technical language and jargon to enhance professionalism
- C. Addressing referral questions and communicating assessment results clearly
- D. Highlighting the student's weaknesses without discussing strengths

Answer:

You have assessed a 12-year-old student with emotional and behavioral challenges. The assessment results reveal a pattern of behavior consistent with anxiety disorder. How should you communicate this finding to the student's parents?

- A. Use vague language to avoid causing unnecessary concern
- B. Be honest and straightforward, providing information and recommendations
- C. Advise the parents to seek help from another professional
- D. Suggest that the student's behavior is typical for their age

Answer:

QUESTION 119

You have conducted an assessment of a 6-year-old student with speech and language difficulties. The assessment results indicate a significant language delay. When writing the assessment report, what is essential to include?

- A. Omit the specific assessment results to avoid overwhelming the parents
- B. Focus on the child's age-expected abilities to maintain a positive tone
- C. Clearly report the assessment results, including strengths and weaknesses
- D. Provide a general summary without discussing specific findings

Answer:

QUESTION 120

You are preparing an assessment report for a 14-year-old student with reading difficulties. The report will be shared with a multidisciplinary team, including teachers and specialists. What should you keep in mind when writing the report to ensure its effectiveness in guiding interventions?

- A. Use technical language to demonstrate expertise
- B. Focus solely on academic test results and omit behavioral observations
- C. Address the referral questions and provide actionable recommendations
- D. Downplay the severity of the reading difficulties to avoid alarming the team

Answer:

QUESTION 121

You have conducted an assessment of a 10-year-old student with suspected learning disabilities. The assessment results show a significant discrepancy between the student's cognitive abilities and academic achievement. How should you communicate this finding in the assessment report?

- A. Avoid discussing the discrepancy to prevent confusion
- B. Highlight the academic achievement as the sole focus of the report
- C. Clearly explain the discrepancy and its implications for intervention planning
- D. Recommend additional assessments without discussing the current findings

Answer:

QUESTION 122

You are part of a schoolwide team focused on promoting mental health among students. After reviewing data, you notice an increase in student stress levels. What is the most effective initial step in addressing this issue?

A. Implementing individual counseling for all students
B. Conducting a schoolwide stress reduction workshop
C. Identifying and addressing stressors through data analysis
D. Ignoring the issue as stress is common among students

Answer:

QUESTION 123

Your school is implementing a schoolwide prevention program to promote healthy eating habits among students. What is a key strategy to ensure the program's success?

A. Providing unhealthy food options to maintain choice
B. Promoting strict dietary restrictions
C. Involving students, parents, and staff in program planning
D. Implementing the program without any input from stakeholders

Answer:

QUESTION 124

Your school has noticed an increase in bullying incidents. As a school psychologist, what collaborative approach can you take to address this issue effectively?

A. Implement a punitive disciplinary approach without consulting other professionals
B. Collaborate with teachers and administrators to develop a comprehensive anti-bullying program
C. Ignore the issue and let students handle it themselves
D. Recommend expulsion for students involved in bullying

Answer:

QUESTION 125

Your school is implementing a physical activity program to improve the physical well-being of students. What is a critical aspect of promoting participation and long-term engagement in this program?

A. Forcing all students to participate in the program
B. Focusing solely on competitive sports
C. Providing a variety of enjoyable physical activities
D. Eliminating physical education classes to prioritize the program

Answer:

QUESTION 126

Your school has identified a significant increase in student absenteeism, which is affecting academic achievement. What collaborative strategy can help address this issue?

A. Implementing a strict attendance policy without input from other professionals
B. Collaborating with teachers, counselors, and families to identify and address the causes of absenteeism
C. Ignoring the issue as absenteeism is a common problem
D. Recommending suspension for students with high absenteeism

Answer:

QUESTION 127

You are reviewing a school's compliance with federal education laws. Which law focuses on improving educational outcomes for all students, including those with disabilities, through various provisions such as accountability and assessment requirements?

- A. Americans with Disabilities Act (ADA)
- B. Elementary and Secondary Education Act (ESEA)
- C. Section 504 of the Rehabilitation Act
- D. Individuals with Disabilities Education Improvement Act (IDEIA)

Answer:

QUESTION 128

You are advocating for a student with a disability who requires reasonable accommodations in a university setting. Which federal law is most relevant to ensure that the student's rights are protected?

- A. Section 504 of the Rehabilitation Act
- B. Individuals with Disabilities Education Improvement Act (IDEIA)
- C. Americans with Disabilities Act (ADA)
- D. Elementary and Secondary Education Act (ESEA)

Answer:

QUESTION 129

A school is not providing reasonable accommodations to a student with a disability, despite repeated requests. What federal law should the student's family reference to enforce their rights to accommodations?

- A. Section 504 of the Rehabilitation Act
- B. Elementary and Secondary Education Act (ESEA)
- C. Individuals with Disabilities Education Improvement Act (IDEIA)
- D. Americans with Disabilities Act (ADA)

Answer:

QUESTION 130

In a mainstream classroom, you observe two students, Sarah and Jake. Sarah has been identified with ADHD, while Jake is a typically developing student of the same age. Both students are struggling with staying focused during lectures. Which of the following is the most appropriate step for you to take in this situation?

- A. Implement a behavior intervention plan specifically for Sarah to address her ADHD symptoms.
- B. Conduct a thorough assessment to identify potential underlying issues affecting both Sarah and Jake's ability to focus.
- C. Assign extra homework to Jake to ensure he catches up with the class.
- D. Recommend a different classroom arrangement for Sarah.

Answer:

QUESTION 131

You are working with a student, Michael, who has been identified with autism spectrum disorder (ASD). Michael excels in mathematics and demonstrates exceptional abilities in this area. How can you best support Michael's educational needs?

- A. Enroll Michael in a special education program for students with ASD to receive targeted support.
- B. Provide opportunities for Michael to engage in advanced mathematics coursework or extracurricular activities.
- C. Ignore Michael's strengths in mathematics and focus solely on addressing his ASD-related challenges.
- D. Encourage Michael to participate in social skills groups to improve his interaction with peers.

Answer:

QUESTION 132

You are working with a kindergarten student, Emily, who has been identified with a specific learning disability in reading. Emily's parents are concerned about her progress and are seeking your advice on how to best support her at home. Which of the following suggestions would be most beneficial for Emily's parents?

- A. Provide Emily with extra reading assignments to improve her reading skills.
- B. Foster a positive reading environment at home by reading aloud to Emily and encouraging her to engage in independent reading for enjoyment.
- C. Enroll Emily in an intensive summer reading program to accelerate her progress.
- D. Restrict Emily's access to non-academic activities until her reading skills improve.

Answer:

QUESTION 133

You are working with a high school student, Alex, who has been identified with emotional and behavioral disorders (EBD). Recently, Alex has been displaying increased aggression towards peers and staff members. Which of the following steps should you take first to address this behavior?

- A. Develop a behavior intervention plan (BIP) with strategies to address Alex's aggression.
- B. Conduct a functional behavior assessment (FBA) to understand the underlying causes of Alex's aggression.
- C. Implement a reward system to reinforce positive behavior in the classroom.
- D. Recommend a change in Alex's academic placement to a more restrictive setting.

Answer:

QUESTION 134

You are working with a student, Lily, who has been identified with a speech and language impairment. Lily's parents are concerned about her social interactions with peers. Which of the following strategies would be most effective in supporting Lily's social development?

- A. Arrange individual playdates for Lily with peers her age to practice social skills in a controlled environment.
- B. Provide speech therapy exclusively focusing on articulation and language development.
- C. Encourage Lily to participate in group activities or clubs that align with her interests.
- D. Limit Lily's interactions with peers to prevent potential conflicts.

Answer:

QUESTION 135

You are working with a middle school student, Ryan, who has been identified with attention-deficit/hyperactivity disorder (ADHD). Ryan's teachers have reported difficulties in managing his impulsive behavior in the classroom. Which of the following interventions would be most effective for addressing Ryan's impulsive behavior?

- A. Implement a daily report card system to monitor and reinforce Ryan's behavior throughout the school day.
- B. Assign additional homework to keep Ryan occupied and focused on academic tasks.
- C. Recommend a change in Ryan's classroom placement to a smaller, more structured environment.
- D. Provide Ryan with a sensory toolkit to use as a self-regulation tool when he feels overwhelmed.

Answer:

QUESTION 136

You are working with a 7th-grade student, Max, who is struggling in his language arts class. After reviewing his assessments, you notice that Max excels in comprehension but struggles with written expression. Which of the following strategies would be most effective in supporting Max's academic progress?

- A. Provide Max with additional reading assignments to further develop his comprehension skills.
- B. Offer Max opportunities for structured writing activities and provide explicit instruction in the writing process.
- C. Enroll Max in a specialized language arts program for advanced learners.
- D. Assign Max to a peer tutoring program to receive assistance from classmates.

Answer:

QUESTION 137

You are working with a kindergarten student, Mia, who has been identified with a speech and language impairment. Mia is struggling to communicate effectively with her peers. She becomes frustrated and often withdraws from social interactions. Which of the following interventions would be most appropriate for Mia?

- A. Enroll Mia in a small group play therapy program to address her social difficulties.
- B. Provide Mia with individual speech therapy sessions focusing solely on articulation.
- C. Implement a social skills curriculum within the classroom to support Mia's interaction with peers.
- D. Restrict Mia's access to group activities to prevent potential communication breakdowns.

Answer:

QUESTION 138

You are working with a 9th-grade student, Sarah, who has a specific learning disability in mathematics. Sarah has made progress in understanding concepts but struggles with applying them in problem-solving situations. What approach would be most effective in supporting Sarah's learning?

- A. Provide Sarah with additional practice problems to reinforce her understanding of mathematical concepts.
- B. Implement strategies that focus on real-world applications of mathematical concepts and problem-solving skills.
- C. Enroll Sarah in an advanced mathematics course to challenge her abilities.
- D. Assign a peer tutor to work with Sarah on homework assignments.

Answer:

QUESTION 139

You are working with a 5th-grade student, Jake, who has been identified with attention-deficit/hyperactivity disorder (ADHD). Jake excels in mathematics but struggles with staying focused during lectures. Which of the following strategies would be most effective in supporting Jake's academic success?

- A. Provide Jake with additional assignments in mathematics to challenge his abilities.
- B. Implement a structured note-taking system and offer breaks for movement during lectures.
- C. Assign Jake to a special education program to receive targeted support for ADHD.
- D. Recommend a change in Jake's classroom placement to a more structured environment.

Answer:

QUESTION 140

You are working with a 6th-grade student, Emily, who is struggling in both language arts and mathematics. After conducting assessments, you discover that Emily has a specific learning disability in reading comprehension. Which of the following interventions would be most effective in addressing Emily's needs?

- A. Enroll Emily in an intensive summer reading program to accelerate her reading skills.
- B. Provide Emily with additional assignments in both language arts and mathematics to improve her overall academic performance.
- C. Implement targeted strategies to improve Emily's reading comprehension skills within the classroom setting.
- D. Recommend placement in a special education program to receive comprehensive support.

Answer:

QUESTION 141

You are working with a 3rd-grade student, Liam, who has been identified with autism spectrum disorder (ASD). Liam struggles with transitions and sensory sensitivities, which impact his ability to participate fully in classroom activities. Which of the following accommodations would be most effective in supporting Liam's academic engagement?

- A. Provide Liam with a visual schedule outlining daily activities and transitions.
- B. Assign Liam to a separate room with reduced sensory stimuli for individualized instruction.
- C. Encourage Liam to participate in extracurricular activities to improve his social skills.
- D. Limit Liam's exposure to group activities to prevent potential overstimulation.

Answer:

QUESTION 142

You are working with a diverse group of students, including English Language Learners (ELLs) who recently joined your school. The school is considering implementing a new assessment tool to measure reading comprehension. What should be a primary consideration when choosing the assessment tool?

- A. The tool's alignment with the school's curriculum and learning objectives.
- B. The cost-effectiveness of the assessment tool.
- C. The popularity of the assessment tool in other schools.
- D. The availability of training materials for the assessment tool.

Answer:

QUESTION 143

You are working with a culturally diverse group of students, each with unique linguistic backgrounds. The school is in the process of selecting an assessment tool to measure mathematical reasoning. What factor should weigh heavily in the decision-making process?

- A. The assessment tool's norming sample and its representation of diverse linguistic backgrounds.
- B. The availability of technical support for administering the assessment.
- C. The length of time required to administer the assessment.
- D. The popularity of the assessment tool in neighboring school districts.

Answer:

QUESTION 144

A school has received a referral for a 4th-grade student, Alex, who is struggling academically. The school previously conducted a comprehensive evaluation for Alex in 2nd grade, which indicated specific learning disabilities. The parents are concerned about Alex's progress and are seeking reevaluation. What should be a priority for the school psychologist in this reevaluation process?

- A. Reviewing the previous evaluation results to identify any changes or trends in Alex's academic performance.
- B. Administering a new battery of assessments to gather additional data on Alex's strengths and needs.
- C. Consulting with Alex's teachers and gathering information on classroom interventions and accommodations that have been implemented.
- D. Recommending a change in Alex's academic placement based on the previous evaluation findings.

Answer:

QUESTION 145

You are working with a group of English Language Learners (ELLs) who have recently arrived at your school. The school is considering using a standardized assessment to measure their reading proficiency. What should be a key consideration when selecting an assessment tool for these students?

- A. The availability of translated versions of the assessment in the students' native languages.
- B. The length of time required to administer the assessment.
- C. The popularity of the assessment tool in neighboring school districts.
- D. The cost-effectiveness of the assessment tool.

Answer:

QUESTION 146

A school has implemented early intervening services for a group of struggling students. After a period of intervention, the school is reviewing their progress. Some students have made significant improvements, while others continue to struggle. What should be the next step for the school in this situation?

- A. Conducting a thorough review of the intervention strategies and adjusting them based on individual student needs.
- B. Continuing with the same intervention strategies, as they have been effective for some students.
- C. Recommending a change in academic placement for students who have not shown improvement.
- D. Discontinuing the intervention services for all students.

Answer:

QUESTION 147

You are working with a diverse group of students, including those from various cultural backgrounds. The school is in the process of selecting an assessment tool for initial referrals. What factor should be a primary consideration in this selection process?

- A. The cultural sensitivity and appropriateness of the assessment tool for the diverse student population.
- B. The cost-effectiveness of the assessment tool.
- C. The availability of technical support for administering the assessment.
- D. The popularity of the assessment tool in neighboring school districts.

Answer:

QUESTION 148

You are tasked with interpreting the results of a cognitive assessment for a 7-year-old student, Emily. Her Full Scale IQ score falls within the Average range. However, there is a significant discrepancy between her verbal and nonverbal scores, with the verbal score being much higher. What should be your primary consideration when interpreting these results?

A. Investigate potential language-related factors that may have influenced Emily's verbal score.
B. Focus on identifying interventions that target Emily's nonverbal cognitive abilities.
C. Disregard the discrepancy and consider Emily's overall Full Scale IQ score as the most accurate representation of her cognitive abilities.
D. Recommend a reevaluation using a different cognitive assessment tool to confirm the results.

Answer:

QUESTION 149

You have administered a reading assessment to a 5th-grade student, James. His scores indicate that he struggles with decoding but excels in reading comprehension. The assessment report provides percentile ranks for both areas. How would you interpret James' performance on this assessment?

A. James is likely to benefit from targeted interventions focused on improving his decoding skills.
B. James' overall reading ability is below grade level, and he may require special education services.
C. James' strengths in reading comprehension compensate for his weaknesses in decoding.
D. James' decoding difficulties may be due to a lack of interest in reading.

Answer:

QUESTION 150

You are reviewing the results of a social-emotional assessment for a 10-year-old student, Alex. The assessment includes scales for self-regulation, social skills, and emotional well-being. Alex scores in the 2nd percentile for self-regulation, 30th percentile for social skills, and 70th percentile for emotional well-being. What would be the most appropriate recommendation based on these results?

A. Implement interventions focused on improving Alex's self-regulation skills.
B. Provide support for developing Alex's social skills within peer interactions.
C. Acknowledge and reinforce Alex's emotional well-being, while monitoring progress in other areas.
D. Suggest a comprehensive intervention plan addressing all three areas simultaneously.

Answer:

QUESTION 151

You have conducted a behavior assessment for a 3rd-grade student, Sarah, who exhibits challenging behaviors in the classroom. The assessment results indicate that Sarah's behavior is influenced by specific triggers and environmental factors. What would be an important next step based on these assessment findings?

A. Develop a behavior intervention plan (BIP) tailored to address Sarah's specific triggers and environmental factors.
B. Provide Sarah with rewards and consequences to modify her behavior.
C. Recommend a change in Sarah's academic placement to a more structured environment.
D. Conduct further assessments to gather additional data on Sarah's behavior.

Answer:

QUESTION 152

You have conducted a comprehensive assessment for a 4-year-old child, Liam, to evaluate his developmental milestones. The assessment results indicate that Liam is below age-level expectations in fine motor skills but on track for other developmental areas. What would be an appropriate recommendation based on these results?

- A. Implement targeted interventions to support Liam's fine motor skill development.
- B. Suggest a comprehensive intervention plan addressing all developmental areas simultaneously.
- C. Monitor Liam's progress without implementing specific interventions at this time.
- D. Recommend a change in Liam's academic placement to a more specialized program.

Answer:

QUESTION 153

You have conducted an assessment of academic achievement for a 6th-grade student, Jake. The results indicate that Jake performs significantly below grade level in mathematics, while his performance in language arts is within the average range for his age. What would be an important consideration when reporting these assessment results to Jake's parents and teachers?

- A. Emphasize Jake's strengths in language arts to provide a balanced perspective of his abilities.
- B. Clearly communicate Jake's performance in mathematics and discuss appropriate interventions and support.
- C. Recommend that Jake be placed in a special education program due to his low performance in mathematics.
- D. Downplay Jake's difficulties in mathematics to avoid causing concern for his parents and teachers.

Answer:

QUESTION 154

You are working with a 4th-grade student, Sarah, who is experiencing frequent anxiety-related symptoms that interfere with her academic performance. Sarah's teacher has reported that she often becomes anxious during math class. Which of the following prevention and intervention strategies would be most appropriate to recommend for Sarah's situation?

- A. Individual counseling sessions to address Sarah's anxiety.
- B. Classroom modifications such as flexible seating arrangements to reduce anxiety triggers.
- C. Group counseling sessions to help Sarah build coping skills with peers.
- D. A change in Sarah's academic placement to a more supportive environment.

Answer:

QUESTION 155

You are working with a middle school student, Jake, who is struggling with anger management issues and disruptive behavior in the classroom. His behavior is negatively affecting his academic progress and relationships with peers. Which prevention and intervention strategy should be prioritized to address Jake's behavior?

- A. Individual counseling sessions to explore the underlying causes of his anger and develop coping strategies.
- B. Implementing a schoolwide positive behavior support program to create a positive school culture.
- C. Group counseling sessions with other students experiencing similar behavioral challenges.
- D. Enforcing strict disciplinary measures to deter disruptive behavior.

Answer:

QUESTION 156

You are working with a 2nd-grade student, Mia, who has been identified with specific learning disabilities in reading and writing. Mia's parents are concerned about her academic progress and want to know how to support her at home. What would be an effective prevention and intervention strategy to recommend for Mia's parents?

- A. Enroll Mia in a specialized reading and writing program outside of school.
- B. Provide Mia with additional assignments in reading and writing to practice at home.
- C. Encourage Mia's parents to read with her regularly and support her in completing homework.
- D. Suggest a change in Mia's academic placement to a more intensive special education program.

Answer:

QUESTION 157

You are working with a high school student, Alex, who is experiencing chronic absenteeism and low academic motivation. After assessing his situation, you find that he has a history of substance abuse and is struggling with depression. Which prevention and intervention strategy should be prioritized to address Alex's situation?

- A. Individual counseling sessions to address his substance abuse and depression.
- B. Implementing a schoolwide attendance incentive program to motivate students to attend regularly.
- C. Group counseling sessions to provide peer support for substance abuse issues.
- D. Recommending expulsion to remove Alex from the school environment.

Answer:

QUESTION 158

You are working with a 6th-grade student, Emily, who is experiencing bullying and social isolation at school. Emily is struggling with low self-esteem and feelings of sadness. Which prevention and intervention strategy should be prioritized to address Emily's situation?

- A. Group counseling sessions to build social skills and foster peer relationships.
- B. Classroom modifications to create a more inclusive and supportive classroom environment.
- C. Individual counseling sessions to address Emily's self-esteem and emotional well-being.
- D. Recommending Emily's transfer to a different school to avoid further bullying.

Answer:

QUESTION 159

You are working with a 5th-grade student, Liam, who is struggling with attention difficulties and impulsivity in the classroom. His teacher reports that these behaviors are hindering his academic progress. Which prevention and intervention strategy should be prioritized to address Liam's behavior?

- A. Implementing a schoolwide behavior management program to provide consistent expectations and rewards.
- B. Enrolling Liam in a specialized program for students with attention difficulties.
- C. Group counseling sessions to teach self-regulation and impulse control skills.
- D. Individual counseling sessions to assess the underlying causes of Liam's behavior.

Answer:

QUESTION 160

A high school student, Mark, has recently experienced the sudden loss of a close family member. He is showing signs of grief and is struggling to cope with his emotions. Mark's teacher has requested your assistance. Which crisis intervention approach should you recommend for Mark at this time?

- A. Group counseling sessions with other students who have experienced a similar loss.
- B. Implementing a schoolwide grief support program to provide a supportive environment.
- C. Individual counseling sessions to address Mark's specific grief reactions and coping strategies.
- D. Referring Mark to an external community service provider for grief counseling.

Answer:

QUESTION 161

You are working with a 7th-grade student, Lily, who is struggling with severe test anxiety. Lily's anxiety is affecting her academic performance and overall well-being. Which counseling and behavioral intervention method should be prioritized to address Lily's test anxiety?

- A. Implementing a schoolwide relaxation and stress management program for all students.
- B. Group counseling sessions to provide support and teach coping strategies for test anxiety.
- C. Individual counseling sessions to assess the underlying causes of Lily's anxiety and develop personalized strategies.
- D. Recommending that Lily's parents take her out of standardized testing to reduce anxiety.

Answer:

QUESTION 162

A middle school is dealing with a crisis situation involving a sudden school lockdown due to a security threat. Students and staff are experiencing heightened anxiety, and parents/guardians are concerned about their children's safety. What is the most appropriate crisis prevention and intervention model to implement during this situation?

- A. Critical Incident Stress Debriefing (CISD) sessions for students, staff, and parents/guardians.
- B. Group counseling sessions for students to discuss their fears and concerns.
- C. Individual counseling sessions for staff members to address their own stress and anxiety.
- D. A schoolwide emergency response plan to ensure physical safety during lockdowns.

Answer:

QUESTION 163

You are working with an elementary school student, Ethan, who frequently exhibits aggressive behavior towards classmates during recess. The school is concerned about the safety of other students. What behavioral intervention method should be prioritized to address Ethan's aggressive behavior?

- A. Implementing a schoolwide positive behavior support program to reinforce positive behaviors.
- B. Group counseling sessions for Ethan to address his aggressive tendencies with peers.
- C. Individual counseling sessions with Ethan to explore the underlying causes of his aggression.
- D. Recommending expulsion to remove Ethan from the school environment.

Answer:

QUESTION 164

A school is facing a crisis situation in which multiple students have been affected by a natural disaster, resulting in significant trauma and emotional distress. School personnel, parents/guardians, and community service providers are all involved in the response efforts. What approach should be taken to effectively collaborate with all stakeholders in this crisis intervention?

- A. Conducting regular meetings with school personnel and community service providers to coordinate efforts.
- B. Group counseling sessions for affected students and their parents/guardians to provide emotional support.
- C. Individual counseling sessions for students to address their trauma and emotional distress.
- D. Prioritizing communication with parents/guardians and limiting involvement of community service providers.

Answer:

QUESTION 165

You are working with a high school student, Olivia, who is experiencing persistent bullying from her peers, leading to emotional distress and a decline in academic performance. Which counseling and behavioral intervention method should be prioritized to address Olivia's situation?

- A. Implementing a schoolwide anti-bullying program to create a safer school environment.
- B. Group counseling sessions with other students who have experienced bullying.
- C. Individual counseling sessions with Olivia to address the emotional distress and develop coping strategies.
- D. Recommending that Olivia change schools to escape the bullying.

Answer:

QUESTION 166

You are working with a parent who is concerned about her child's academic progress. The parent is expressing frustration and feels overwhelmed by the situation. What approach should you take to promote effective communication with this parent?

- A. Actively listen to the parent's concerns, validate her feelings, and offer support and guidance.
- B. Quickly provide solutions to address the academic concerns and offer reassurance.
- C. Suggest enrolling the child in additional extracurricular activities to improve academic performance.
- D. Recommend that the parent seek a second opinion from an outside professional.

Answer:

QUESTION 167

You are working with a 5th-grade student, Jack, who has difficulty expressing his emotions verbally. Jack often becomes frustrated when trying to communicate his feelings. What alternative communication mode could be effective for Jack?

- A. Visual communication tools such as emotion cards or a feelings chart.
- B. Providing written prompts for Jack to express his emotions through written words.
- C. Suggesting that Jack use nonverbal cues such as gestures to convey his feelings.
- D. Encouraging Jack to communicate exclusively through verbal means to build his confidence.

Answer:

QUESTION 168

You are working with a diverse group of students, including English Language Learners (ELLs) and students with speech and language disabilities. What communication mode would be most effective in ensuring clear and accessible communication for this group?

- A. Utilizing visual aids and written instructions to support verbal communication.
- B. Relying solely on verbal communication to encourage language acquisition for ELLs.
- C. Incorporating complex vocabulary and sentences to challenge language skills.
- D. Utilizing advanced technological communication devices for all students.

Answer:

QUESTION 169

You have been tasked with facilitating a meeting involving school personnel, parents, and community professionals to discuss a student's Individualized Education Program (IEP). The meeting is expected to address the student's specific needs and goals. What communication skills should you prioritize in this scenario?

- A. Active listening, clear articulation of ideas, and the ability to facilitate productive discussions.
- B. Providing brief, one-way communication to efficiently cover all necessary information.
- C. Minimizing parent involvement to streamline the meeting process.
- D. Relying solely on written communication for clarity.

Answer:

QUESTION 170

You are working with a student, Emily, who is on the autism spectrum and benefits from visual supports. What communication mode would be most effective in providing instructions and information to Emily?

A. Using visual schedules, charts, and diagrams to supplement verbal instructions.
B. Relying solely on verbal communication to encourage Emily's verbal skills.
C. Incorporating complex vocabulary and detailed explanations to challenge Emily's comprehension.
D. Utilizing advanced technological communication devices for all instructions.

Answer:

QUESTION 171

You are working with a group of parents from diverse cultural backgrounds who have varying levels of English proficiency. What communication mode would be most effective in ensuring that all parents receive and understand important information?

A. Providing translated written materials and offering interpreters for important meetings or events.
B. Relying solely on verbal communication in English to encourage language acquisition.
C. Utilizing advanced technological communication devices for all interactions.
D. Minimizing written communication to avoid potential language barriers.

Answer:

QUESTION 172

You have received a referral for a 3rd-grade student, Alex, who is struggling academically. The teacher has observed difficulties with attention and behavior in the classroom. As the school psychologist, what is your initial role in this situation?

A. Conducting a functional-behavioral assessment to understand the underlying factors contributing to Alex's difficulties.
B. Serving as a case manager for the assessment process, coordinating with relevant stakeholders.
C. Recommending immediate special education placement based on the teacher's observations.
D. Conducting a research study to investigate effective interventions for similar cases.

Answer:

QUESTION 173

You have been invited to participate in a multidisciplinary team meeting to discuss a student's Individualized Education Program (IEP). What is a key responsibility of the school psychologist in this meeting?

A. Providing recommendations for instructional strategies and accommodations to support the student's needs.
B. Making decisions about the student's educational placement without consulting other team members.
C. Focusing solely on behavioral assessments, excluding other aspects of the student's development.
D. Leaving the meeting early if there are no specific concerns related to your area of expertise.

Answer:

QUESTION 174

You are conducting a research study to evaluate the effectiveness of a new intervention program for students with reading difficulties. What is a crucial step in this research process?

A. Gathering baseline data on the students' reading abilities before implementing the intervention.
B. Conducting individual counseling sessions for the participating students.
C. Providing immediate feedback to teachers regarding the effectiveness of the intervention program.
D. Recommending changes to the program based on initial observations.

Answer:

QUESTION 175

A high school student, Sarah, is experiencing severe behavioral difficulties in the classroom. Her teacher has requested a functional-behavioral assessment. What is a critical step in conducting this assessment?

- A. Observing Sarah's behavior in various settings and situations to identify triggers and patterns.
- B. Conducting academic assessments to determine if there are underlying learning difficulties.
- C. Recommending immediate expulsion due to the severity of Sarah's behavioral difficulties.
- D. Initiating group counseling sessions for Sarah to address her behavioral challenges.

Answer:

QUESTION 176

You have been asked to assist school administrators in problem-solving and decision-making regarding a student with complex needs. What approach should you take in this situation?

- A. Collaborate with the administrators to gather relevant data and information on the student's needs.
- B. Provide a unilateral recommendation based on your own assessment without consulting the administrators.
- C. Focus solely on academic assessments, neglecting other aspects of the student's development.
- D. Delegate the responsibility to another staff member, as this is primarily an administrative task.

Answer:

QUESTION 177

You have been assigned as the case manager for a reevaluation of a student with specific learning disabilities. What is a key responsibility in this role?

- A. Coordinating with relevant stakeholders to gather updated assessment data and input.
- B. Recommending immediate changes to the student's academic placement without consultation.
- C. Conducting group counseling sessions to address the student's learning difficulties.
- D. Focusing solely on previous assessment data and neglecting the need for updated information.

Answer:

QUESTION 178

You have received a referral for a 6th-grade student, Michael, who is struggling academically. The teacher believes he may have a learning disability. What is the appropriate next step based on state policies and procedures?

- A. Conduct a comprehensive evaluation to determine if Michael meets eligibility criteria for special education services.
- B. Immediately recommend special education placement based on the teacher's referral.
- C. Suggest additional tutoring sessions for Michael to address academic difficulties.
- D. Advise the teacher to implement more challenging curriculum to address Michael's academic needs.

Answer:

QUESTION 179

You are reviewing a case where a student, Emily, has been identified as eligible for special education services due to a specific learning disability. What is a key responsibility of the school psychologist in this situation?

- A. Collaborating with the IEP team to develop and implement an appropriate Individualized Education Program (IEP) for Emily.
- B. Recommending changes to the student's educational placement without consulting the IEP team.
- C. Conducting group counseling sessions for students with learning disabilities.
- D. Focusing solely on academic assessments, neglecting other aspects of Emily's development.

Answer:

QUESTION 180

You have been informed of a case where a student, David, is facing disciplinary action due to behavior violations. According to state policies and procedures, what is a crucial consideration in this situation?

- A. Ensuring that David's rights to due process and procedural safeguards are upheld throughout the disciplinary process.
- B. Expediting the disciplinary process to quickly address David's behavior.
- C. Recommending immediate suspension without a formal review process.
- D. Minimizing communication with David's parents to maintain confidentiality.

Answer:

QUESTION 181

You are working in a diverse school district with students from various cultural backgrounds. What is an important consideration when applying state policies to ensure equity for all students?

- A. Recognizing and respecting the cultural differences and unique needs of students and their families.
- B. Applying a one-size-fits-all approach to policies to maintain consistency.
- C. Avoiding any reference to cultural background to maintain impartiality.
- D. Recommending the same interventions for all students regardless of their cultural background.

Answer:

QUESTION 182

You are working with a student, Sarah, who has recently moved to a new state and is transitioning into a new school district. What is a critical step in ensuring a smooth transition for Sarah, in accordance with state policies?

- A. Reviewing Sarah's educational records and conducting any necessary assessments to determine appropriate placement and services.
- B. Recommending that Sarah repeat a grade level to ensure a seamless transition.
- C. Ignoring Sarah's previous educational experiences to start fresh in the new district.
- D. Focusing solely on Sarah's social and emotional adjustment, neglecting academic considerations.

Answer: A

Explanation: State policies require a review of a student's educational records and, if necessary, assessments to determine appropriate placement and services when transitioning to a new school district.

QUESTION 183

You have been asked to participate in a committee reviewing graduation requirements for the district. What is a key responsibility of the school psychologist in this committee?

- A. Advocating for equitable graduation requirements that consider the diverse needs of all students.
- B. Enforcing strict graduation requirements without flexibility for individual circumstances.
- C. Focusing solely on academic criteria for graduation, neglecting other aspects of student development.
- D. Recommending changes to graduation requirements without consulting other committee members.

Answer:

QUESTION 184

You are working with a 10-year-old student who is struggling with emotional regulation. Their parents report frequent tantrums and difficulty managing frustration. You suspect that a lack of self-awareness might be contributing to these issues. Which of the following strategies would be most effective for promoting emotional development in this student?

- A. Implementing a strict behavior management system with clear consequences.
- B. Encouraging the student to journal their thoughts and feelings regularly.
- C. Assigning extra academic tasks to keep the student busy and distracted.
- D. Reducing the student's access to all forms of media and screen time.

Answer:

QUESTION 185

You are working with a group of preschool children in a diverse classroom setting. To promote their cognitive development, which of the following activities would be most effective?

- A. Providing identical learning materials for all children.
- B. Encouraging children to engage in open-ended, imaginative play.
- C. Assigning specific roles to children during group activities.
- D. Focusing exclusively on individualized instruction.

Answer:

QUESTION 186

You are working with a high school student who has a history of academic underachievement and low self-esteem. Which of the following approaches is most likely to promote their academic and emotional development?

- A. Assigning more homework and additional study hours.
- B. Providing frequent praise and constructive feedback.
- C. Isolating the student from their peers during class.
- D. Reducing access to extracurricular activities.

Answer:

QUESTION 187

You are working with a 6-year-old student who exhibits delayed language development. Which of the following interventions is most suitable for promoting their language and communication development?

- A. Limiting verbal interactions to encourage the use of nonverbal communication.
- B. Encouraging the child to spend more time alone with electronic devices.
- C. Engaging the child in conversation and reading books together regularly.
- D. Reducing exposure to social situations to minimize communication challenges.

Answer:

QUESTION 188

You are working with a high school student with a strong interest in technology but struggles with reading comprehension. Which instructional approach is most appropriate to enhance their reading skills while capitalizing on their technology interests?

- A. Assigning traditional paper-based reading assignments.
- B. Providing audiobooks without any written material.
- C. Encouraging the student to explore interactive e-books.
- D. Focusing solely on oral discussions without written content.

Answer:

QUESTION 189

You are working with an elementary school student who excels in math but struggles with social interactions. To promote their effective functioning in various school settings, which strategy is most appropriate?

- A. Assigning additional math assignments to further enhance their math skills.
- B. Enrolling the student in social skills training sessions.
- C. Encouraging the student to work independently on math projects.
- D. Reducing opportunities for social interactions to minimize challenges.

Answer:

QUESTION 190

You are working with a middle school student who struggles with attention and focus during traditional classroom instruction. To enhance their learning opportunities, what instructional modification would be most appropriate?

- A. Increasing the length of classroom lectures.
- B. Providing written notes only as study materials.
- C. Incorporating interactive and hands-on activities.
- D. Reducing the complexity of the curriculum.

Answer:

QUESTION 191

You are working with a group of high school students with diverse learning needs. To identify appropriate recommendations for curriculum and instructional modifications, which approach should you prioritize?

- A. Implementing a one-size-fits-all curriculum to maintain consistency.
- B. Individualizing curriculum and instruction based on each student's needs.
- C. Excluding students with exceptional needs from mainstream classrooms.
- D. Focusing solely on standardized testing to gauge student progress.

Answer:

QUESTION 192

You are part of a multidisciplinary team assessing a 5-year-old child for special education services. The child's teacher reports concerns about their speech and language development. Which assessment model is most appropriate for gathering information to address these concerns?

- A. Conducting a traditional standardized language assessment.
- B. Administering a general cognitive assessment.
- C. Observing the child's interactions during playtime.
- D. Relying solely on parent interviews.

Answer:

QUESTION 193

You are assessing a high school student with a suspected learning disability in mathematics. The student has struggled with math throughout their academic career. What type of assessment procedure is most appropriate to directly inform interventions for this student?

- A. Conducting a one-time standardized math test.
- B. Administering a comprehensive math achievement battery.
- C. Observing the student's participation in math class.
- D. Interviewing the student's peers about their math abilities.

Answer:

QUESTION 194

You are working with a group of elementary school students who struggle with reading comprehension. Which dynamic assessment procedure is most appropriate to directly inform interventions for this group?

- A. Administering a timed reading comprehension test.
- B. Conducting an informal reading assessment with no intervention.
- C. Implementing a scaffolded reading comprehension assessment.
- D. Relying on standardized reading comprehension scores.

Answer:

QUESTION 195

You are part of a multidisciplinary team evaluating a 10-year-old student for special education services. The student exhibits challenging behaviors in the classroom. What assessment approach should you prioritize to make appropriate educational placement and programming recommendations?

- A. Relying on teacher-reported behavior logs.
- B. Administering a brief personality assessment.
- C. Conducting a functional behavior assessment.
- D. Reviewing the student's medical records.

Answer:

QUESTION 196

You are working with a preschool-aged child with suspected speech and language delays. Which assessment model would best help you provide information to address referral questions and make appropriate educational recommendations for this child?

- A. Administering a general developmental assessment.
- B. Conducting a parent interview about the child's communication.
- C. Observing the child's interactions during group play.
- D. Utilizing a standardized articulation test.

Answer:

QUESTION 197

You are tasked with assessing a student from a culturally diverse background for giftedness. The student excels in mathematics but struggles in language arts. What is the most appropriate approach to determine the presence and nature of their giftedness?

- A. Relying solely on standardized achievement test scores.
- B. Conducting a comprehensive, culturally sensitive assessment.
- C. Focusing on the student's strengths in mathematics only.
- D. Utilizing a teacher's recommendation as the primary source of data.

Answer:

QUESTION 198

You are working with a student who consistently achieves top scores on standardized tests but displays uneven performance in the classroom. Some teachers have noted a lack of motivation and engagement. What critical factor should you consider in assessing this student's giftedness?

- A. Relying solely on the student's standardized test scores.
- B. Assessing the student's motivation and creativity.
- C. Consulting with teachers for their opinions.
- D. Focusing exclusively on the student's academic achievements.

Answer:

QUESTION 199

You are tasked with identifying gifted students in a culturally diverse school setting. What is the most important reason to ensure that your assessment tools and procedures are culturally fair and unbiased?

- A. To meet legal requirements for educational assessments.
- B. To provide equal opportunities for all students to be identified.
- C. To maintain consistency with school district policies.
- D. To reduce the need for individualized testing accommodations.

Answer:

QUESTION 200

You are working with a student who comes from a culturally and linguistically diverse background. The student's English language skills are limited, but they demonstrate exceptional mathematical abilities. Which assessment approach should you prioritize to determine the nature of their giftedness?

- A. Conducting a standardized English language proficiency test.
- B. Administering a culturally sensitive assessment of mathematical skills.
- C. Relying on teacher observations and recommendations.
- D. Focusing on the student's lack of English proficiency.

Answer:

QUESTION 201

You are working with a 5th-grade student who has been identified as gifted in mathematics but is experiencing social and emotional challenges in the general education classroom. Which educational placement and service option would be most appropriate to address this student's needs?

- A. Placing the student in a self-contained gifted education classroom.
- B. Providing counseling services within the general education classroom.
- C. Implementing Response to Intervention (RTI) for mathematics.
- D. Recommending an Individualized Education Program (IEP) for social and emotional support.

Answer:

QUESTION 202

You are working with a 1st-grade student who has a diagnosed speech and language disorder. The student struggles to communicate effectively with peers and teachers. What educational placement and service option is most appropriate to address this student's needs?

- A. Placing the student in a general education classroom with speech therapy.
- B. Enrolling the student in a special education classroom for speech and language disorders.
- C. Implementing an Individualized Family Service Plan (IFSP) for speech therapy.
- D. Recommending extended-year services to address the communication disorder.

Answer:

QUESTION 203

You are working with a high school student who has a documented learning disability in reading. Despite receiving targeted interventions through Response to Intervention (RTI), the student continues to struggle. What educational placement and service option should you consider next?

- A. Transitioning the student to a general education classroom without additional support.
- B. Recommending an Individualized Education Program (IEP) with specialized reading instruction.
- C. Extending Response to Intervention (RTI) services for a longer duration.
- D. Placing the student in a self-contained special education classroom.

Answer:

QUESTION 204

You are working with a student who has a medical condition that requires frequent monitoring and care during the school day. Which educational placement and service option should you recommend to address the student's health needs while allowing them to access the general education curriculum?

- A. Developing an Individualized Health Care Plan (IHCP) for the student.
- B. Placing the student in a self-contained special education classroom with a nurse.
- C. Extending the school day to provide more time for medical care.
- D. Recommending enrollment in a gifted education program.

Answer:

QUESTION 205

You are working with a 3rd-grade student who is an English Language Learner (ELL) and has been identified as gifted in mathematics. What educational placement and service option would be most appropriate to address this student's unique combination of needs?

- A. Placing the student in an English as a Second Language (ESL) program with additional math support.
- B. Enrolling the student in a self-contained gifted education classroom.
- C. Implementing Response to Intervention (RTI) for English language proficiency.
- D. Recommending an Individualized Education Program (IEP) with differentiated math instruction.

Answer:

QUESTION 206

You are working with a middle school student who is experiencing significant anxiety and academic difficulties. The student's parents have limited financial resources and no health insurance. Which resource would be most appropriate for addressing the student's psychological and academic needs while considering their financial situation?

- A. Referring the student to a private therapist who specializes in anxiety disorders.
- B. Connecting the student with the school's guidance counselor for counseling services.
- C. Exploring community-based mental health clinics that offer sliding-scale fees.
- D. Recommending an out-of-district alternative school for specialized support.

Answer:

QUESTION 207

You are working with a high school student who exhibits disruptive behavior in the classroom. The student's behavior negatively impacts their academic performance and relationships with peers and teachers. What resource or service should you prioritize to address this behavioral issue?

- A. Enrolling the student in a private therapeutic school.
- B. Recommending a school-based behavior intervention plan.
- C. Referring the student to a local after-school program.
- D. Exploring academic tutoring services.

Answer:

QUESTION 208

You are working with an elementary school student who is struggling with reading and has been identified as at risk for learning disabilities. The student's parents are seeking additional academic support. What resource should you recommend to provide academic assistance?

- A. Encouraging the parents to hire a private tutor.
- B. Referring the student to a local community center for homework help.
- C. Suggesting the student attend a summer camp for reading improvement.
- D. Recommending the school's Response to Intervention (RTI) program.

Answer:

QUESTION 209

You are working with a high school student who is dealing with substance abuse issues. The student's parents are looking for external resources to address this problem. What resource or service should you suggest to the student's parents?

A. Recommending individual therapy with a private psychologist.
B. Encouraging the student to join a local sports team.
C. Referring the student to the school's guidance counselor.
D. Suggesting the student attend a community-based support group for teens.

Answer:

QUESTION 210

You are working with an elementary school student who is experiencing frequent health issues and missing a significant amount of school. The student's parents are concerned about their education. What resource or service should you recommend to address the student's health-related school absences?

A. Suggesting the parents hire a private tutor for home schooling.
B. Referring the student to a local youth sports program.
C. Encouraging the parents to seek medical advice from a specialist.
D. Recommending the school's Individualized Health Care Plan (IHCP) team.

Answer:

QUESTION 211

You are working as a school psychologist, and the school district has recently implemented a new technology-based system for tracking student progress and behavior. However, many teachers and staff are struggling to use the system effectively. What consultative and collaborative approach should you employ to promote change and help staff adapt to the new technology?

A. Conducting workshops focused solely on the technical aspects of the system.
B. Collaborating with a small group of tech-savvy teachers to train others.
C. Facilitating a series of training sessions that emphasize both technical skills and practical application.
D. Encouraging teachers to seek external resources independently.

Answer:

QUESTION 212

You are part of a consultation team tasked with improving classroom management practices in a local school district. The team includes teachers, administrators, and educational specialists. What consultative and collaborative skill should you prioritize to facilitate change at the district level?

A. Focusing on individual teacher training and development.
B. Promoting top-down decision-making and policy changes.
C. Engaging in open and transparent communication among team members.
D. Limiting collaboration to within specific grade levels or departments.

Answer:

QUESTION 213

You are collaborating with a group of parents, teachers, and administrators to address student bullying issues within a school district. Parents have expressed concerns about their children's safety. What consultative and collaborative skill should you prioritize to communicate clearly with this diverse audience?

- A. Providing parents with technical documentation on bullying prevention measures.
- B. Using complex terminology and educational jargon to convey the seriousness of the issue.
- C. Listening actively to parents' concerns and using plain language to explain prevention strategies.
- D. Limiting communication to written reports shared with school administrators only.

Answer:

QUESTION 214

You are working as a school psychologist in a district where there is resistance to changes in teaching methods aimed at improving student outcomes. How can you utilize consultative and collaborative skills to promote change at the classroom level effectively?

- A. Advocating for change without involving teachers in decision-making.
- B. Implementing new methods without seeking input from teachers.
- C. Collaborating with teachers to understand their concerns and needs.
- D. Providing one-time training sessions with no follow-up support.

Answer:

QUESTION 215

You are consulting with a group of school administrators and policy makers to address the challenges of improving student attendance rates. There are differing opinions on the causes and solutions. What consultative and collaborative skill is crucial to navigate this situation successfully?

- A. Advocating for a single, predetermined solution.
- B. Encouraging policy makers to make unilateral decisions.
- C. Facilitating open and constructive dialogue among stakeholders.
- D. Excluding teachers and students from the discussion.

Answer:

QUESTION 216

You are a school psychologist working with a school district that is considering implementing a new discipline policy to address behavior problems. The proposed policy involves strict punitive measures for all students who violate rules. However, some educators and parents are concerned about its potential negative impact on students. What is the most appropriate approach to assist in designing a discipline policy that is effective and fair?

- A. Advocating for the immediate implementation of the proposed policy to maintain order.
- B. Conducting a comprehensive review of research on effective discipline practices.
- C. Defending the proposed policy without considering alternative approaches.
- D. Consulting only with teachers and administrators and excluding parents and students.

Answer:

QUESTION 217

You are working with a school district to improve their staff development program. What critical aspect of school systems should you consider when designing and implementing effective staff development initiatives?

- A. Implementing a one-size-fits-all training program for all staff members.
- B. Ensuring that staff development focuses solely on technical skills.
- C. Tailoring staff development to address the specific needs of different staff members.
- D. Conducting staff development in isolation from the broader educational context.

Answer:

QUESTION 218

You are a school psychologist in a district where grading policies are under review due to concerns about consistency and fairness. Some teachers advocate for strict adherence to traditional grading practices, while others suggest more flexible approaches. What key factor should you consider when assisting in the evaluation of grading policies?

- A. Preserving traditional grading practices to maintain consistency.
- B. Advocating for the strict implementation of one grading approach.
- C. Balancing consistency with flexibility to meet diverse student needs.
- D. Excluding teacher input and relying solely on administrative decisions.

Answer:

QUESTION 219

You are collaborating with a school district to enhance their special education services. What is a fundamental aspect of the organization and operation of school systems that you should consider when designing and implementing improved special education programs?

- A. Isolating special education services from general education.
- B. Focusing solely on academic accommodations for students with disabilities.
- C. Promoting inclusive practices that integrate students with disabilities into general education settings.
- D. Implementing separate policies and practices for students with disabilities.

Answer:

QUESTION 220

You are assisting a school district in developing a comprehensive staff development program. The district serves a diverse student population, including English Language Learners (ELLs). What critical factor should you consider when designing staff development initiatives to support ELL students?

- A. Focusing solely on staff development for ELL specialists.
- B. Ignoring cultural and linguistic diversity in staff development.
- C. Incorporating strategies that address the unique needs of ELL students.
- D. Isolating ELL students from general education initiatives.

Answer:

QUESTION 221

When evaluating the effectiveness of a school intervention program aimed at improving reading skills, what is a critical consideration in data-based decision making?

- A. Relying solely on standardized test scores as the primary measure of success.
- B. Using a variety of data sources and measures to assess program outcomes.
- C. Disregarding data that do not show immediate improvement.
- D. Prioritizing qualitative data over quantitative data.

Answer:

QUESTION 222

You are conducting a program evaluation for a school district to assess the impact of a new bullying prevention program. The program has been in place for one year, and initial data shows a decrease in reported bullying incidents. However, there are concerns about the program's long-term effectiveness. What data-based decision-making principle should guide your evaluation in this situation?

- A. Concluding that the program is successful based on one year of data.
- B. Continuously monitoring and evaluating the program over time.
- C. Disregarding concerns and focusing solely on short-term outcomes.
- D. Relying on anecdotal evidence to assess program effectiveness.

Answer:

QUESTION 223

You are tasked with conducting research to assess the factors contributing to student absenteeism in a school district. What research method should you employ to gather in-depth insights into this issue?

- A. Administering a standardized test to measure student attendance.
- B. Conducting surveys with teachers and parents about student absenteeism.
- C. Analyzing historical attendance data for patterns and trends.
- D. Observing students' attendance behaviors in the classroom.

Answer:

QUESTION 224

You are part of a school improvement team tasked with making data-based decisions to enhance student performance in mathematics. The team has identified a need for professional development for math teachers. What principle of data-based decision making should guide the selection of professional development strategies?

- A. Choosing professional development based on personal preferences of teachers.
- B. Providing professional development without considering specific student needs.
- C. Tailoring professional development to address specific student performance data.
- D. Offering a single, standardized professional development program for all teachers.

Answer:

QUESTION 225

When conducting program evaluations in schools, what ethical consideration is essential to uphold during data collection and analysis?

- A. Prioritizing the interests of the research team over the welfare of students.
- B. Focusing exclusively on quantitative data to ensure objectivity.
- C. Protecting the privacy and confidentiality of student and staff information.
- D. Excluding stakeholders, such as parents and teachers, from the evaluation process.

Answer:

QUESTION 226

You are a school psychologist working with a middle school student, Alex, who has been displaying disruptive behavior in the classroom. You have observed that Alex frequently talks out of turn, refuses to follow classroom rules, and often disrupts the learning environment for others. Which intervention strategy is most appropriate for addressing Alex's disruptive behavior?

- A. Implementing a behavior modification plan that includes rewards for positive behavior and consequences for disruptive behavior.
- B. Recommending immediate suspension from school to send a strong message to Alex and deter future disruptions.
- C. Conducting a one-on-one counseling session with Alex to explore the underlying causes of the disruptive behavior.
- D. Assigning extra homework and detention as punishment for each disruptive incident.

Answer:

QUESTION 227

As a school psychologist, you have been asked to address bullying behavior in a high school. You have conducted interviews with students and staff and collected data on bullying incidents. What is the most appropriate next step in addressing this issue?

- A. Organizing an assembly to publicly shame the bullies and discourage their behavior.
- B. Developing a comprehensive anti-bullying program that includes education, prevention, and intervention components.
- C. Ignoring the issue since bullying is a common problem in high schools, and it will eventually resolve itself.
- D. Isolating the bullies by placing them in separate classrooms to prevent further harm to their victims.

Answer:

QUESTION 228

You are working with a group of elementary school students who are struggling with social skills and forming positive peer relationships. They often engage in conflicts, have difficulty sharing, and struggle to communicate effectively with their peers. Which intervention approach is most appropriate for helping these students develop better social skills?

- A. Conducting individual counseling sessions with each student to address their social difficulties.
- B. Organizing group therapy sessions to teach social skills and practice them in a supportive setting.
- C. Assigning more homework related to social skills development.
- D. Ignoring the issue as children will naturally outgrow these social challenges.

Answer:

QUESTION 229

You are a school psychologist working with a high school student, Sarah, who is experiencing symptoms of anxiety and stress related to academic performance. Sarah frequently worries about exams, experiences physical symptoms of anxiety, and has trouble concentrating in class. Which intervention technique is most appropriate for helping Sarah manage her academic-related anxiety?

- A. Encouraging Sarah to avoid school and academic-related activities to reduce stress.
- B. Providing Sarah with relaxation and mindfulness techniques to manage anxiety.
- C. Ignoring Sarah's concerns as they are a normal part of the high school experience.
- D. Increasing Sarah's academic workload to help her overcome her anxiety.

Answer:

QUESTION 230

You are working with a student, Emily, who has been struggling academically in mathematics. After conducting a thorough assessment, you find that Emily's math difficulties stem from a specific deficit in number sense. Which assessment tool would be most appropriate to further evaluate Emily's number sense and guide intervention?

- A. A standardized achievement test in mathematics to assess Emily's overall math performance.
- B. A comprehensive neuropsychological assessment to explore all possible cognitive factors affecting Emily's learning.
- C. A curriculum-based assessment focusing on Emily's performance on current math curriculum objectives.
- D. A specialized number sense assessment designed to target the specific deficit area.

Answer:

QUESTION 231

You are working with a high school student, Daniel, who has a documented reading disability. To determine appropriate interventions, you need to assess Daniel's reading abilities. Which type of assessment is most suitable for assessing Daniel's reading skills?

- A. A group-administered reading comprehension test to compare Daniel's performance to his peers.
- B. An individually administered diagnostic reading assessment to identify specific areas of difficulty.
- C. A general intelligence test to gauge Daniel's overall cognitive abilities.
- D. A teacher's observation of Daniel's reading behavior in the classroom.

Answer:

QUESTION 232

You are assisting a team in selecting an assessment tool for a student, Alex, who has limited English proficiency. The team is interested in evaluating Alex's language proficiency in both English and his native language, Spanish. Which assessment approach would be most appropriate for assessing Alex's language proficiency in both languages?

- A. Administering a single assessment in English to measure overall language proficiency.
- B. Using a translated version of a standardized language assessment in English.
- C. Conducting a bilingual assessment that includes assessments in both English and Spanish.
- D. Relying on teacher and parent interviews to assess Alex's language skills.

Answer:

QUESTION 233

You are working with a student, Maria, who has a visual impairment. Maria's parents are concerned about her educational progress. To assess her reading abilities, which assessment adaptation would be most appropriate for Maria?

- A. Providing Maria with large-print versions of standardized reading assessments.
- B. Using an oral assessment format where Maria responds verbally to reading comprehension questions.
- C. Requesting Maria to complete written assessments with the assistance of a magnifying glass.
- D. Administering a tactile assessment that uses Braille materials.

Answer:

QUESTION 234

You are a school psychologist working as part of a multidisciplinary team for a student, James, who is struggling academically and showing signs of anxiety. The team has gathered assessment data on James's academic performance and emotional well-being. Based on the data, which intervention approach is most appropriate for James?

- A. Implementing individual counseling sessions to address James's academic and emotional concerns separately.
- B. Collaborating with teachers to provide academic accommodations without addressing his emotional needs.
- C. Integrating academic support with social-emotional interventions to address both aspects simultaneously.
- D. Recommending a medication evaluation to address James's anxiety.

Answer:

QUESTION 235

You are part of a multidisciplinary team assessing a student, Sarah, who has difficulty with attention and concentration in the classroom. Sarah's teachers and parents have provided input, and you've conducted assessments that indicate attention-related challenges. What is the most appropriate next step in the multidisciplinary team process for Sarah?

- A. Initiating medication treatment for attention-related issues without further assessment.
- B. Developing an Individualized Education Plan (IEP) with academic accommodations only.
- C. Conducting additional assessments to identify the underlying causes of Sarah's attention difficulties.
- D. Recommending counseling sessions to address Sarah's attention and behavioral concerns.

Answer:

QUESTION 236

You are working with a multidisciplinary team to develop interventions for a student, Alex, who is experiencing severe test anxiety. The team has reviewed assessment data and identified the need for interventions. Which intervention strategy would be most effective in addressing Alex's test anxiety?

- A. Providing extra time and a separate room for Alex during exams to reduce anxiety.
- B. Encouraging Alex to study harder and use test-taking strategies independently.
- C. Implementing a systematic desensitization program to gradually expose Alex to test-like situations.
- D. Recommending medication to manage Alex's test anxiety.

Answer:

QUESTION 237

You are part of a multidisciplinary team assessing a student, Mia, who is struggling with reading comprehension. The team has conducted various assessments and identified weaknesses in her phonemic awareness skills. What is the most appropriate intervention approach for Mia based on the assessment findings?

- A. Providing Mia with additional reading comprehension exercises to improve her overall reading skills.
- B. Implementing targeted phonemic awareness interventions to strengthen her foundational reading skills.
- C. Recommending Mia for speech therapy to address any potential speech-related issues.
- D. Advising Mia's parents to enroll her in a specialized reading program.

Answer:

QUESTION 238

Sarah, a 5-year-old kindergarten student, has been struggling with her reading skills. She often becomes frustrated in the classroom and has difficulty concentrating during reading activities. Her teacher has noticed that Sarah is also having trouble making friends and frequently isolates herself during recess. Sarah's parents are concerned about her behavior. As a school psychologist, which of the following statements best reflects the interrelationship between Sarah's struggles in the cognitive and social/emotional domains?

- A. Sarah's reading difficulties are likely causing her social isolation because she feels embarrassed in front of her peers.
- B. Sarah's social isolation is likely causing her reading difficulties because she lacks peer support and motivation.
- C. Sarah's difficulties in both reading and social interactions may be indicative of a broader developmental issue.
- D. Sarah's reading difficulties and social isolation are unrelated, and each should be addressed separately.

Answer:

QUESTION 239

Which of the following statements best demonstrates an understanding of the interrelationship between cognitive and language development in children?

- A. Cognitive development primarily influences language development, with language skills dependent on cognitive milestones.
- B. Language development primarily influences cognitive development, as language skills are essential for logical thinking.
- C. Cognitive and language development are mutually influential, with each domain supporting and enhancing the other.
- D. Cognitive development and language development occur independently and do not significantly impact each other.

Answer:

QUESTION 240

Jake, a 12-year-old student, excels academically but often displays aggressive behavior towards his peers during recess. He struggles to control his anger and has been involved in several conflicts. Which of the following statements best reflects the potential interrelationship between Jake's cognitive and social/emotional development?

- A. Jake's aggressive behavior is a result of his high academic achievement, which causes him to feel superior to his peers.
- B. Jake's aggressive behavior is unrelated to his cognitive development; it may be attributed to external factors.
- C. Jake's advanced cognitive abilities may contribute to his frustration when his peers do not meet his intellectual expectations.
- D. Jake's aggressive behavior is a sign of a developmental delay in both cognitive and social/emotional domains.

Answer:

QUESTION 241

Which of the following scenarios best illustrates how changes in the social/emotional domain can affect performance in the cognitive domain?

- A. Emma's improved social skills have led to better classroom behavior and focus during math lessons.
- B. Liam's struggles with anger management have not impacted his academic performance.
- C. Sophia's strong cognitive abilities have resulted in excellent social interactions with peers.
- D. Daniel's shyness in social situations has no bearing on his academic performance.

Answer:

QUESTION 242

Sarah, a 10-year-old student, has recently moved to a new school. She is struggling academically and often seems disinterested in class. As a school psychologist, which of the following factors affecting students' learning is most likely contributing to Sarah's difficulties?

- A. Biological factors related to her brain development
- B. Socioeconomic status of her family
- C. Teacher expectations
- D. Cultural or ethnic background

Answer:

QUESTION 243

Which of the following best reflects an understanding of how psychopathological factors can affect students' learning?

- A. Psychopathological factors primarily affect a student's ability to form friendships but have little impact on academic performance.
- B. Psychopathological factors can significantly disrupt a student's emotional and cognitive functioning, impairing both social and academic development.
- C. Psychopathological factors mainly influence a student's physical health but do not affect their learning abilities.
- D. Psychopathological factors are irrelevant in understanding students' learning difficulties.

Answer:

QUESTION 244

David, a 6-year-old student, frequently exhibits impulsive behavior in the classroom, such as interrupting the teacher and not following instructions. Which factor affecting students' learning is most likely contributing to David's behavior?

A. Biological factors related to his temperament
B. Cultural or ethnic background
C. Family issues
D. Teacher expectations

Answer:

QUESTION 245

Which of the following statements best demonstrates an understanding of the role of family issues in students' learning?

A. Family issues have no impact on a student's academic performance if the school environment is supportive.
B. Family issues can affect a student's learning by influencing their motivation and home environment.
C. Family issues are solely responsible for a student's academic success or failure.
D. Family issues only affect a student's physical health, not their academic abilities.

Answer:

QUESTION 246

Maria, a 14-year-old student, consistently receives low grades in mathematics. She often expresses a lack of interest in the subject and struggles to complete her math assignments. As a school psychologist, which of the following factors affecting students' learning is most likely contributing to Maria's difficulties in math?

A. Socioeconomic status
B. Parent expectations
C. Student motivation
D. Prenatal and early environment

Answer:

QUESTION 247

Sarah, a 7-year-old student, is struggling in her first-grade class. Her teacher has noticed that she frequently avoids reading aloud and appears anxious during reading activities. As a school psychologist, which type of assessment instrument would be most appropriate to gather information about Sarah's reading difficulties in a non-threatening way?

A. Standardized reading comprehension test
B. Structured observation of her reading behavior
C. Multiple-choice quiz on reading comprehension
D. Teacher interview about Sarah's reading habits

Answer:

QUESTION 248

Which of the following statements best describes the benefits of using curriculum-based assessments (CBA) in the evaluation of students' academic progress?

A. CBAs are best suited for identifying students' cognitive development milestones.
B. CBAs provide a comprehensive overview of students' mental health and adaptive skills.
C. CBAs offer frequent and direct assessment of students' academic skills within their classroom context.
D. CBAs are primarily designed for diagnosing learning disabilities.

Answer:

QUESTION 249

James, a 10-year-old student, has been identified as having difficulties in his social and emotional development. His teacher has observed disruptive behavior in the classroom. Which type of assessment instrument would be most appropriate for evaluating James's social and emotional development and identifying specific areas of concern?

- A. IQ test
- B. Standardized achievement test in mathematics
- C. Behavioral checklist completed by the teacher
- D. Parent interview about James's family background

Answer:

QUESTION 250

When selecting an assessment instrument for evaluating the progress of a school-age student with a suspected learning disability, which of the following factors should a school psychologist consider most critically?

- A. The popularity and reputation of the assessment instrument
- B. The cost of the assessment instrument
- C. The validity and reliability of the assessment instrument for the specific student population
- D. The availability of online resources for the assessment instrument

Answer:

QUESTION 251

Emily, a 4-year-old preschooler, is showing delays in her language development. Her parents are concerned and have sought assistance. As a school psychologist, which type of assessment instrument would be most appropriate to gather information about Emily's language development and potential speech delays?

- A. Standardized intelligence test
- B. Parent interview about Emily's family history
- C. Speech and language assessment conducted by a speech therapist
- D. Multiple-choice vocabulary test

Answer:

QUESTION 252

Julia, a 12-year-old student with a visual impairment, is scheduled for a cognitive assessment. Which adaptation should a school psychologist consider to ensure an appropriate assessment for Julia?

- A. Administering the assessment in a well-lit room
- B. Providing the assessment in braille or using assistive technology
- C. Offering additional time for completing the assessment
- D. Including a sensory break during the assessment

Answer:

QUESTION 253

Which of the following best reflects an understanding of how procedural modifications for administering standardized assessments can affect assessment results?

- A. Procedural modifications may have no impact on assessment results if the content of the assessment remains unchanged.
- B. Procedural modifications can significantly alter assessment results and should be avoided.
- C. Procedural modifications can make assessments more accessible without affecting the validity of results.
- D. Procedural modifications are unnecessary and should not be considered when administering standardized assessments.

Answer:

QUESTION 254

Alex, a 6-year-old student with attention deficit hyperactivity disorder (ADHD), is scheduled for an academic assessment. Which procedural modification should a school psychologist consider to accommodate Alex's needs during the assessment?

A. Providing extra time for completing the assessment
B. Allowing breaks during the assessment
C. Administering the assessment in a group setting
D. Using a shorter version of the assessment

Answer:

QUESTION 255

When administering an assessment to a student who requires special education services, which of the following considerations is essential to ensure the assessment's validity?

A. Administering the assessment in a quiet room to minimize distractions
B. Adhering strictly to the standardized procedures outlined in the assessment manual
C. Making modifications to the assessment to accommodate the student's individual needs
D. Encouraging the student to complete the assessment independently without assistance

Answer:

QUESTION 256

Michael, a 9-year-old student with dyslexia, is scheduled for a reading assessment. Which procedural modification should a school psychologist consider to accommodate Michael's needs during the assessment?

A. Providing the assessment in a larger font size
B. Administering the assessment orally
C. Reducing the number of assessment items
D. Extending the time limit for completing the assessment

Answer:

QUESTION 257

Emily, a 7-year-old student, has been referred for a cognitive assessment due to concerns about her academic performance. Emily is an English language learner (ELL) from a non-English-speaking background. She has been in an English-speaking school for two years. As a school psychologist, you are tasked with conducting the assessment. Which procedural consideration should you prioritize to ensure a fair and accurate cognitive assessment for Emily?

A. Administer the assessment in English only, as it aligns with the school's language of instruction.
B. Translate the assessment into Emily's native language to ensure she fully comprehends the content.
C. Extend the time limit for Emily to compensate for language processing differences.
D. Use visual aids to supplement verbal instructions during the assessment.

Answer:

QUESTION 258

Daniel, a 10-year-old student, has been identified as having attention deficit hyperactivity disorder (ADHD). He is scheduled for a standardized reading assessment. Daniel's ADHD symptoms include impulsivity and difficulty sustaining attention. As a school psychologist, what procedural modification should you implement to accommodate Daniel's needs during the assessment?

- A. Administer the assessment in a quiet room to minimize distractions.
- B. Allow Daniel to take breaks during the assessment when needed.
- C. Provide the assessment in a smaller font size to improve readability.
- D. Use a shorter version of the assessment to reduce the testing time.

Answer:

QUESTION 259

Sarah, a 9-year-old student, is scheduled for an academic assessment. She has a documented learning disability that affects her reading fluency and comprehension. Sarah's teacher has reported that she often struggles to finish reading assignments within the allotted time. As a school psychologist, how should you adapt the assessment to ensure an accurate evaluation of Sarah's reading abilities?

- A. Provide Sarah with additional time to complete the assessment.
- B. Use a different assessment that does not involve reading.
- C. Assess Sarah's reading abilities without any accommodations.
- D. Provide Sarah with a peer reader to assist her during the assessment.

Answer:

Chapter 2 – Answers and Explanations

QUESTION 1

Answer: D

Explanation: A key component of promoting mental health is educating students, staff, and parents about mental health and available resources. This reduces stigma, increases awareness, and ensures that individuals know how to seek help when needed. Options A, B, and C do not adequately address mental health promotion.

QUESTION 2

Answer: C

Explanation: The first step in designing an effective intervention plan is to conduct a comprehensive assessment to understand the student's specific needs and challenges in reading comprehension. This assessment provides the necessary data to tailor the intervention appropriately.

QUESTION 3

Answer: B

Explanation: Evaluating the efficacy of a behavior intervention program involves collecting data regularly throughout the intervention period. This ongoing data collection allows for the monitoring of progress, adjustment of strategies, and assessment of effectiveness over time.

QUESTION 4

Answer: B

Explanation: One of the key advantages of using technology for progress monitoring is the ability to collect and analyze data in real-time. This allows for timely adjustments to interventions and better-informed decision-making.

QUESTION 5

Answer: B

Explanation: The primary focus of evaluating the outcomes of a schoolwide anti-bullying program should be to examine changes in bullying rates and behaviors over time. This approach allows for data-driven conclusions about program effectiveness rather than relying on anecdotal reports or general impressions.

QUESTION 6

Answer: C

Explanation: When implementing a data-driven decision-making system, it is crucial to ensure data accuracy and reliability. Decision-making based on inaccurate or unreliable data can lead to ineffective interventions and accountability issues.

QUESTION 7

Answer: B

Explanation: A critical step in assessing the impact of a math intervention program is to collect baseline data before the intervention begins. This baseline data provides a comparison point for evaluating the effectiveness of the program and tracking student progress over time.

QUESTION 8

Answer: B

Explanation: The first step in involving the family effectively in the education process is to schedule a meeting to discuss their concerns and perspectives. This approach demonstrates respect for the family's input and helps build a collaborative partnership.

QUESTION 9

Answer: C

Explanation: A key principle when organizing a family engagement event is to ensure that it is culturally sensitive and inclusive. This approach promotes meaningful engagement among diverse families and respects their cultural backgrounds and perspectives.

QUESTION 10

Answer: B

Explanation: An effective strategy for involving a family with limited English proficiency is to provide translated materials and offer interpreters during meetings. This ensures effective communication and engagement while respecting language barriers.

QUESTION 11

Answer: B

Explanation: A critical aspect of promoting collaboration between families and educators is to encourage open communication and active listening. Effective collaboration involves valuing the input and perspectives of all stakeholders, including families.

QUESTION 12

Answer: B

Explanation: To encourage family involvement in the intervention process, it is recommended to provide information about the importance of family involvement and its benefits. This can help alleviate hesitations and motivate families to participate.

QUESTION 13

Answer: C

Explanation: A key focus of a workshop on effective family-school partnerships should be to highlight the benefits of collaborative relationships between families and educators. This approach promotes the understanding of the positive impact of family involvement on student success.

QUESTION 14

Answer: C

Explanation: IDEIA ensures that students with disabilities have access to a free appropriate public education (FAPE) tailored to their individual needs. While other laws like ADA and Section 504 provide protections, IDEIA specifically addresses educational services for students with disabilities.

QUESTION 15

Answer: C

Explanation: ADA prohibits discrimination on the basis of disability in various settings, including public schools. It ensures equal access and protection against discrimination for individuals with disabilities.

QUESTION 16

Answer: C

Explanation: IDEIA mandates the provision of appropriate educational services to students with disabilities through the development and implementation of IEPs. It provides legal mechanisms for enforcing these services and ensuring that students receive the support they need.

QUESTION 17

Answer: C

Explanation: Based on the assessment data, Emma exhibits significant deficits in both academic skills (reading and mathematics) and displays symptoms of anxiety and low self-esteem. Therefore, the most appropriate recommendation is that Emma should receive special education services to address both her academic and emotional needs.

QUESTION 18

Answer: A

Explanation: Based on the assessment data, Tyler exhibits significant difficulties in reading fluency and comprehension, which affect his academic performance. While his cognitive abilities are within the average range, his reading difficulties meet the eligibility criteria for special education services under the category of Specific Learning Disability (SLD).

QUESTION 19

Answer: A

Explanation: Based on the assessment data that indicates a severe speech and language impairment significantly impacting Ethan's communication skills, the most appropriate recommendation is that Ethan should receive special education services to address his speech and language impairment. This aligns with eligibility criteria for services under the category of Speech or Language Impairment.

QUESTION 20

Answer: B

Explanation: An IFSP primarily focuses on addressing the needs and goals of children in early childhood intervention services. It is a family-centered plan that outlines the services and supports to help children like Emily with developmental delays reach their developmental milestones.

QUESTION 21

Answer: A

Explanation: The annual goals and objectives are the components of an IEP that are specifically designed to address the student's educational needs and goals. These goals outline what the student is expected to achieve over the course of the year and guide instructional planning.

QUESTION 22

Answer: C

Explanation: In John's IEP, the annual goals and objectives should be carefully considered to address his specific needs related to reading comprehension and written expression. These goals will outline the specific skills and outcomes that John should work towards during the school year to improve his reading and writing abilities.

QUESTION 23

Answer: C

Explanation: The related services component of an IEP typically outlines the specific services and support that a student with a disability will receive to help them achieve their educational goals. These services may include speech therapy, occupational therapy, counseling, and other specialized supports tailored to the student's needs.

QUESTION 24

Answer: C

Explanation: In Sarah's IEP, the related services component should be given particular attention to address her sensory sensitivities. Related services such as occupational therapy or sensory interventions can provide targeted support to help Sarah manage sensory sensitivities, which in turn can contribute to her overall success in the educational setting.

QUESTION 25

Answer: C

Explanation: When a student like Mark is not making significant progress toward their IEP goals, it is crucial to review and revise the instructional strategies and interventions. The IEP team, including the school psychologist, should collaborate to identify more effective strategies and interventions that better meet Mark's learning needs. Simply increasing the goals' challenge (option A) or the frequency of progress monitoring (option B) may not address the underlying issue. Discontinuing the IEP (option D) is not appropriate when the student still requires support for their specific learning disability.

QUESTION 26

Answer: C

Explanation: To address Emily's continued struggles with attention and self-regulation despite making progress, the IEP team, including the school psychologist, should consider ensuring better alignment between the IEP goals and classroom strategies. This may involve collaborating with the teacher to identify and implement specific strategies and accommodations that can support Emily's success in the classroom. Adjusting the goals (option A) may not be necessary if she is already making progress. Providing additional related services (option B) may not be the most appropriate step at this stage. Removing the goals (option D) is not recommended when the student still requires support.

QUESTION 27

Answer: B

Explanation: To determine the effectiveness of the reading intervention program, you should use a paired-samples t-test. This statistical procedure allows you to compare the reading scores of the same group of students before and after the intervention, assessing whether there is a statistically significant improvement in their reading skills.

QUESTION 28

Answer: C

Explanation: A longitudinal design would be most appropriate for assessing the impact of a classroom behavior management program over time. This design involves collecting data from the same group of students at multiple time points, allowing for the analysis of changes in behavior patterns over an extended period, which is essential for evaluating the program's effectiveness.

QUESTION 29

Answer: C

Explanation: Qualitative research would be the most appropriate research methodology for gathering in-depth insights into students' experiences and perceptions of the counseling services. Qualitative methods, such as interviews or focus groups, allow for a rich exploration of students' perspectives and the factors that contribute to their well-being, providing valuable qualitative data for program evaluation.

QUESTION 30

Answer: C

Explanation: When selecting an assessment instrument for program evaluation, a primary consideration should be the reliability and validity of the assessment instrument. It is crucial to ensure that the instrument measures the intended constructs (in this case, social and emotional development) accurately and consistently to provide valid data for the evaluation. While factors like popularity, cost, and administration time are important, they should not take precedence over the instrument's reliability and validity.

QUESTION 31

Answer: B

Explanation: The most appropriate next step in the consultation and collaboration process is to share the assessment findings and proposed interventions with Sarah's teacher and seek their input and collaboration. Collaboration with the teacher is crucial for the successful implementation of behavioral interventions and ensures that the teacher is actively involved in addressing Sarah's challenges.

QUESTION 32

Answer: C

Explanation: Actively listening to parents' concerns and involving them in the problem-solving process is a critical aspect of maintaining effective communication and collaboration. Collaboration with parents should be a two-way process where their input is valued, and their concerns are addressed, leading to a more productive partnership in supporting the student.

QUESTION 33

Answer: B

Explanation: In this situation, the most appropriate course of action is to collaboratively explore alternative strategies and resources that can support the implementation of the interventions. Effective collaboration involves problem-solving together to find practical solutions that work within the existing context, even when resources are limited. Ignoring the teacher's concerns (option A), recommending independent funding (option C), or referring the student to another school (option D) do not promote effective collaboration.

QUESTION 34

Answer: C

Explanation: To ensure effective integration of a new assessment tool into your practice, it is essential to conduct thorough research on the tool. This includes evaluating its reliability, validity, and appropriateness for your specific context. Jumping directly into using the tool without this evaluation (option A) or sharing it without investigation (option B) can lead to unverified and potentially unreliable practices. Attending more conferences (option D) may provide additional information but does not guarantee the suitability of the tool for your needs.

QUESTION 35

Answer: B

Explanation: Ongoing learning ensures that school psychologists remain up-to-date with the latest research and best practices. Professional development is not solely about maintaining employment (option A) or relevant only for new school psychologists (option C). School psychologists, like professionals in many fields, benefit from continuous learning to provide the best services to students.

QUESTION 36

Answer: B

Explanation: The most effective way to share the discovery of a new technology platform and encourage its adoption among colleagues is to conduct a hands-on workshop to demonstrate the platform's functionality and benefits. This interactive approach allows colleagues to experience the platform firsthand and ask questions, increasing their likelihood of adopting it. Simply sharing an email (option A) or mentioning it briefly in a staff meeting (option C) may not provide enough information or motivation for adoption. Keeping the discovery to oneself (option D) does not align with the collaborative nature of professional development and knowledge sharing in education.

QUESTION 37

Answer: D

Explanation: In this scenario, the student's disruptive behavior and possible drug use are indicative of psychopathological variables. Assessing the student's mental health and potential underlying psychological issues is essential for understanding and addressing the behavior.

QUESTION 38

Answer: C

Explanation: The child's limited language development is likely influenced by their biological temperament, which can affect their communication skills and language acquisition.

QUESTION 39

Answer: D

Explanation: The student's socioeconomic status is a significant variable that can impact their access to basic needs like food and rest, which can, in turn, affect their behavior and development.

QUESTION 40

Answer: D

Explanation: The history of domestic violence in the student's family is a family issue that can significantly contribute to the student's aggressive behavior towards peers.

QUESTION 41

Answer: C

Explanation: Teacher expectations can influence a student's academic performance. Low teacher expectations can lead to underperformance, even in students without learning disabilities.

QUESTION 42

Answer: D

Explanation: High parental and teacher expectations can create pressure on students, potentially leading to emotional struggles and outbursts in class.

QUESTION 43

Answer: B

Explanation: Students with ADHD often benefit from a learning environment that allows for individualized pacing and reduced distractions, which can be better provided through small, self-paced online courses.

QUESTION 44

Answer: C

Explanation: To support a student with ASD's unique needs, a special education classroom with tailored interventions and strategies designed for ASD is likely to be more effective than inclusion in a regular classroom.

QUESTION 45

Answer: A

Explanation: Visual aids and written instructions can help students with auditory processing disorders better comprehend and retain information, making this modification more appropriate for their needs.

QUESTION 46

Answer: C

Explanation: Positive behavior reinforcement, along with a token system, can help motivate and encourage positive behavior in students with behavioral challenges while creating a structured and supportive classroom environment.

QUESTION 47

Answer: B

Explanation: For a student with test anxiety, providing relaxation techniques before assessments can help reduce anxiety levels and improve their ability to perform well during tests.

QUESTION 48

Answer: C

Explanation: A collaborative and inclusive classroom environment can help a student struggling with low self-esteem and social isolation build positive social interactions and improve their emotional well-being.

QUESTION 49

Answer: C

Explanation: Emma, who has dyslexia, would benefit most from targeted reading interventions that address her specific learning needs. Placing her in a small group reading intervention class can provide the necessary support and tailored instruction to help her overcome her reading challenges.

QUESTION 50

Answer: C

Explanation: Students with ADHD often benefit from a quiet and structured learning environment that minimizes distractions. This modification can help Alex stay focused and manage his impulsive behavior more effectively.

QUESTION 51

Answer: C

Explanation: Encouraging peer-assisted learning and group projects can help Liam gradually build his confidence and social skills in a supportive and structured environment. This approach promotes social interaction while respecting his comfort level.

QUESTION 52

Answer: A

Explanation: Test-retest reliability is crucial when selecting an assessment instrument because it indicates the stability and consistency of the test scores over time. For assessing a student's reading abilities, the instrument should yield consistent results on repeated measurements.

QUESTION 53

Answer: A

Explanation: When working with culturally diverse students, it is crucial to choose an assessment tool for which normative data is available for the specific cultural group being assessed. This ensures that the assessment accurately reflects the performance of students from diverse backgrounds.

QUESTION 54

Answer: A

Explanation: Gender bias in an assessment occurs when the test systematically favors one gender over another, leading to inaccurate results. School psychologists should be particularly cautious of gender bias to ensure fair and equitable assessment practices.

QUESTION 55

Answer: C

Explanation: When assessing a child with limited English proficiency, it is crucial to use culturally and linguistically appropriate assessment tools and techniques that consider the child's language and cultural background. This ensures a fair and accurate assessment of their abilities.

QUESTION 56

Answer: C

Explanation: Construct validity is essential when selecting an assessment tool to ensure that it accurately measures the intended construct, in this case, social-emotional development. It assesses whether the test measures the underlying psychological trait or concept it is intended to measure.

QUESTION 57

Answer: B

Explanation: Beneficence emphasizes the psychologist's duty to promote the well-being and best interests of the child. In this case, establishing rapport and ensuring a comfortable testing environment aligns with the ethical principle of beneficence, as it aims to benefit the child's emotional well-being during the assessment process.

QUESTION 58

Answer: B

Explanation: To ensure nondiscriminatory assessment for culturally diverse students, including ELLs, it is essential to provide appropriate accommodations that support their understanding and participation in the assessment while maintaining fairness.

QUESTION 59

Answer: C

Explanation: To ensure accurate assessment results for a student with a hearing impairment who primarily communicates through sign language, it is essential to use sign language interpreters and provide assessments in sign language to accurately evaluate their abilities and needs.

QUESTION 60

Answer: C

Explanation: To ensure accurate and useful assessment results for students with limited English proficiency, it is crucial to use assessments in the student's native language when possible and appropriate. This approach respects linguistic diversity and provides more accurate data.

QUESTION 61

Answer: C

Explanation: To ensure accurate assessment results for a student with a severe visual impairment, using tactile or Braille-based assessments as needed is essential. These specialized methods accommodate the student's unique needs and provide meaningful information for planning instruction and modifications.

QUESTION 62

Answer: C

Explanation: To ensure nondiscriminatory assessments and useful information for instructional planning, it is essential to use assessment measures that consider linguistic and cultural diversity. This approach promotes fairness and accuracy in the assessment process.

QUESTION 63

Answer: C

Explanation: When assessing students from low socioeconomic backgrounds, it is crucial to offer a supportive and empathetic testing environment that takes into account their economic challenges. This approach fosters a more comfortable and equitable assessment experience.

QUESTION 64

Answer: B

Explanation: To ensure fair and accurate assessment for students with limited English proficiency and diverse linguistic backgrounds, it is crucial to utilize interpreters and translated assessments in their native languages. This approach respects their linguistic diversity while providing a valid assessment of their abilities.

QUESTION 65

Answer: C

Explanation: When working with a student with physical disabilities, it is essential to select or adapt assessments that are accessible and measure their cognitive abilities accurately. This approach ensures that the assessments provide meaningful information despite the student's motor difficulties.

QUESTION 66

Answer: D

Explanation: To provide equitable assessments for students from low socioeconomic backgrounds, it is essential to offer a supportive and understanding testing environment that considers their economic challenges. This approach fosters a more comfortable and fair assessment experience while respecting their circumstances.

QUESTION 67

Answer: A

Explanation: Scoring below average on a reading assessment suggests that the student may have a specific learning disability in reading. However, further assessment and evaluation are needed to confirm this diagnosis and develop appropriate interventions.

QUESTION 68

Answer: B

Explanation: The assessment data suggest that while the student performs well on cognitive assessments, they are struggling with emotional regulation and social interactions. This indicates a potential emotional or social disorder that should be further assessed and addressed.

QUESTION 69

Answer: B

Explanation: Significant attention difficulties and hyperactivity suggest the possibility of ADHD or a similar condition. Further assessment and evaluation are necessary to confirm the diagnosis and determine appropriate interventions.

QUESTION 70

Answer: C

Explanation: The assessment data suggest a potential issue with test anxiety that may be impacting the student's academic performance. It is important to explore strategies to address this anxiety and support the student in test-taking situations.

QUESTION 71

Answer: C

Explanation: The assessment data suggest that the student's aggressive behavior is specific to the school environment. Further assessment and exploration are needed to understand the underlying causes and develop appropriate interventions.

QUESTION 72

Answer: B

Explanation: Inconsistent academic performance, with strengths in some subjects and struggles in others, may indicate a specific learning disability affecting certain areas. Further assessment and evaluation are necessary to determine the specific nature of the learning disability and appropriate interventions.

QUESTION 73

Answer: B

Explanation: Based on the functional-behavioral assessment, the most appropriate step is to develop a BIP that includes targeted strategies to address the student's disruptive behavior during challenging math tasks. This approach focuses on addressing the underlying causes of the behavior and providing support within the least restrictive environment.

QUESTION 74

Answer: C

Explanation: The primary consideration for determining placement within the least restrictive environment should be the student's unique learning needs and the potential for inclusion in general education settings. The focus should be on providing the most appropriate educational setting that meets the student's needs while considering inclusion opportunities.

QUESTION 75

Answer: B

Explanation: Based on the student's progress in communication skills, the least restrictive environment should involve placement in a general education classroom with additional support and accommodations. This placement allows the student to access the general education curriculum while receiving the necessary support for social interactions.

QUESTION 76

Answer: B

Explanation: Once the functional-behavioral assessment has identified the triggers and patterns of behavior, the next step is to identify appropriate alternative behaviors that can replace the aggression. This is a critical component of developing a behavior intervention plan (BIP) that promotes positive behavior within the least restrictive environment.

QUESTION 77

This question is intentionally removed.

QUESTION 78

This question is intentionally removed.

QUESTION 79

This question is intentionally removed.

QUESTION 80

Answer: B

Explanation: Given Maria's severe intellectual disability and the need for constant support, a placement in a separate special education classroom for students with severe intellectual disabilities may be the most appropriate option within the continuum of the least restrictive environment while still providing the necessary support.

QUESTION 81

Answer: B

Explanation: When presenting research findings to teachers and parents, it is essential to use plain language and real-life examples to make the information accessible and understandable. This approach ensures that the audience can grasp the relevance and practical implications of the research.

QUESTION 82

Answer: C

Explanation: Data-based decision making involves using multiple sources of data to draw comprehensive conclusions. In the context of evaluating an intervention program, combining pre- and post-assessments with teacher observations and other data sources provides a more accurate and robust understanding of the program's effectiveness.

QUESTION 83

Answer: C

Explanation: When disseminating research findings to district administrators, providing a comprehensive report that includes recommendations is essential. This approach not only presents the research but also offers actionable steps to address the identified issue, facilitating data-based decision making.

QUESTION 84

Answer: C

Explanation: When presenting research findings to parents and the public, it is crucial to prepare a clear and concise presentation that highlights key findings and their implications. This approach ensures that the information is accessible and understandable to a broad audience.

QUESTION 85

Answer: B

Explanation: In a contentious consultation meeting, active listening and empathy are crucial interpersonal skills. These skills help build rapport, facilitate understanding, and de-escalate conflicts by showing respect for diverse perspectives.

QUESTION 86

Answer: C

Explanation: To address conflict arising from cultural differences, it is essential to facilitate open and respectful discussions about cultural diversity and its impact on teaching practices. This approach encourages understanding and collaboration while valuing diverse perspectives.

QUESTION 87

Answer: B

Explanation: To address concerns about discipline and cultural insensitivity, the most appropriate course of action is to acknowledge the parents' concerns and work collaboratively with them to develop a discipline policy that respects cultural diversity. This approach values parental input and promotes a more inclusive disciplinary approach.

QUESTION 88

Answer: B

Explanation: The psychologist's role in this consultation process is to facilitate open and respectful discussions that allow educators to explore different strategies and reach a consensus. This approach values diverse perspectives and encourages collaboration to improve student engagement.

QUESTION 89

Answer: C

Explanation: To help teachers navigate conflicts with parents from culturally diverse backgrounds, the psychologist should emphasize conflict resolution strategies that consider cultural sensitivity and empathy. These skills promote effective communication and understanding, leading to more productive interactions.

QUESTION 90

Answer: B

Explanation: The historical foundation of psychology has evolved to recognize the significance of acknowledging and addressing trauma as a crucial aspect of psychological well-being. School psychologists should approach trauma counseling with this understanding, aiming to support students through their traumatic experiences.

QUESTION 91

Answer: B

Explanation: In cases involving mandated reporting of child abuse or neglect, school psychologists are ethically and legally obligated to report suspicions promptly, even if the facts are not yet fully confirmed. This principle prioritizes the safety and well-being of the child.

QUESTION 92

Answer: C

Explanation: When conducting assessments, school psychologists should prioritize ethical and legal considerations, including ensuring that the assessment is valid and culturally sensitive. This approach promotes fair and equitable assessment practices.

QUESTION 93

Answer: B

Explanation: The primary ethical and professional responsibility in this situation is to provide immediate support to the student and report the bullying incident according to legal and ethical requirements. This approach prioritizes the student's safety and well-being.

QUESTION 94

Answer: B

Explanation: In situations involving a student's disclosure of suicidal thoughts, school psychologists have an ethical and legal duty to ensure the student's safety. This includes notifying the student's parents or guardians to provide immediate support and intervention.

QUESTION 95

Answer: C

Explanation: Medication for ADHD is primarily used to alleviate symptoms and improve focus, rather than curing the disorder or enhancing other cognitive or social skills.

QUESTION 96

Answer: B

Explanation: When a gifted student underachieves, providing enrichment activities is an appropriate strategy to challenge and engage the student further. Suspecting a learning disability or immediately accelerating the student may not be the best course of action.

QUESTION 97

Answer: C

Explanation: Medication is not a standard treatment for specific learning disabilities like dyslexia. Instead, educational interventions and specialized teaching methods are typically employed.

QUESTION 98

Answer: B

Explanation: The school psychologist's role includes monitoring the student's medication compliance and collaborating with other professionals to support the student's overall well-being. Determining medication dosage is the responsibility of a physician, and it is not appropriate for a school psychologist to encourage a student to stop taking prescribed medication.

QUESTION 99

Answer: C

Explanation: Providing sensory accommodations like noise-canceling headphones can help students with ASD manage sensory sensitivities without the need for medication. While other interventions may be appropriate in some cases, sensory accommodations are a direct response to sensory sensitivities.

QUESTION 100

Answer: C

Explanation: A common characteristic of giftedness in the language domain is advanced vocabulary and early reading skills. Gifted children in this domain typically show precocious language development rather than delayed milestones or difficulty in forming social relationships.

QUESTION 101

Answer: A

Explanation: Reducing sensory stimulation to a minimum can help create a more comfortable learning environment for a student with ASD, as it minimizes triggers for sensory sensitivities. Completely eliminating sensory stimuli may not be feasible, and ignoring sensitivities is not an effective strategy.

QUESTION 102

Answer: B

Explanation: Providing a quiet and organized homework space can help a student with attention difficulties focus and complete assignments more effectively. Assigning more homework may overwhelm the student, reducing assignments may not adequately challenge them, and stricter consequences may not address the underlying issue.

QUESTION 103

Answer: B

Explanation: Offering audiobooks and text-to-speech software can help a student with a specific learning disability in reading access and comprehend written materials more effectively. The other options are not suitable for addressing the reading difficulty.

QUESTION 104

Answer: B

Explanation: Providing clear behavior expectations and positive reinforcement is a proactive strategy that can help reduce aggressive behaviors by promoting positive alternatives. Zero-tolerance policies, isolation, and punishment are not effective in addressing the underlying causes of such behaviors.

QUESTION 105

Answer: C

Explanation: Emphasizing consistency in using intervention strategies across different settings is a key principle of generalization. This ensures that the child can apply their learned skills and behaviors in various environments. The other options are not in line with the principle of generalization.

QUESTION 106

Answer: C

Explanation: Providing appropriate support and accommodations in the mainstream classroom is a crucial consideration when facilitating the transition of a student from special education to mainstream. This ensures that the student can access the curriculum and succeed in the new environment. The other options are not recommended strategies for a successful transition.

QUESTION 107

Answer: B

Explanation: In Sarah's case, providing her with a quiet and organized workspace is the most beneficial modification. This helps create an environment conducive to concentration and reduces distractions, which can be particularly helpful for students with ADHD. The other options may not effectively address her specific needs and could potentially worsen the situation.

QUESTION 108

Answer: C

Explanation: The key principle for helping Ethan generalize his social communication skills is to encourage practice and support in various unstructured social settings. This principle aligns with the concept of generalization, which involves applying skills learned in one context to other relevant contexts. Restricting his social interactions or removing him from unstructured settings would not promote generalization.

QUESTION 109

Answer: C

Explanation: To facilitate the transfer of Olivia's math skills, it is crucial to promote collaboration between the resource room teacher and the regular math teacher. This allows for continuity in teaching methods and support across different environments. Options A, B, and D would not support successful transfer and may even hinder her progress.

QUESTION 110

Answer: B

Explanation: A Full-Scale IQ score of 85 falls below the average range, which typically has a mean of 100 and a standard deviation of 15. Therefore, the student's cognitive abilities are below average.

QUESTION 111

Answer: A

Explanation: With a mean score of 75 and a standard deviation of 10, a score of 85 is above the mean, indicating that the student's performance is above average.

QUESTION 112

Answer: A

Explanation: A percentile rank of 75 means that the student scored higher than 75% of the students in the norming group, indicating above-average performance.

QUESTION 113

Answer: B

Explanation: A grade-equivalent score of 4.5 indicates that the child's reading abilities are equivalent to those of an average 5th grader. It is important to note that grade-equivalent scores do not represent the child's chronological age.

QUESTION 114

Answer: B

Explanation: A z-score of -1.5 indicates that the student's performance is 1.5 standard deviations below the mean, signifying below-average performance.

QUESTION 115

Answer: B

Explanation: With a standard deviation of 5, a score of 10 is 2 standard deviations below the mean. This indicates that the student's performance is below average.

QUESTION 116

Answer: A

Explanation: As a school psychologist, it is important to communicate assessment results clearly to parents. Option A is the best choice, as it involves providing a detailed but jargon-free explanation of the assessment result, ensuring that parents can understand the issue and its implications for their child's learning.

QUESTION 117

Answer: C

Explanation: The primary focus when preparing an assessment report should be to address the referral questions and communicate assessment results clearly. This ensures that the report serves its intended purpose of guiding interventions and providing valuable information to the multidisciplinary team.

QUESTION 118

Answer: B

Explanation: It is important to be honest and straightforward when communicating assessment findings related to a potential anxiety disorder. Providing information and recommendations can help parents understand the situation and make informed decisions about interventions or further assessment.

QUESTION 119

Answer: C

Explanation: In an assessment report, it is essential to clearly report the assessment results, including both strengths and weaknesses. This comprehensive approach provides a balanced understanding of the child's abilities and informs appropriate interventions.

QUESTION 120

Answer: C

Explanation: When writing an assessment report for a multidisciplinary team, it is essential to address the referral questions and provide actionable recommendations. This ensures that the report serves as a useful guide for designing appropriate interventions and support strategies.

QUESTION 121

Answer: C

Explanation: When a significant discrepancy is identified in an assessment, it is important to clearly explain the discrepancy and its implications for intervention planning. This information helps the multidisciplinary team understand the student's needs and plan appropriate interventions.

QUESTION 122

Answer: C

Explanation: The most effective initial step is to identify and address the specific stressors causing the increase in stress levels. Data analysis can help pinpoint the underlying issues and inform targeted interventions. Options A and B are broad and may not address the root causes, while option D neglects the problem.

QUESTION 123

Answer: C

Explanation: Involving students, parents, and staff in program planning ensures that the program is tailored to the needs and preferences of the school community. Collaboration and engagement of stakeholders are essential for the success of schoolwide prevention programs.

QUESTION 124

Answer: B

Explanation: Collaborating with teachers and administrators to develop a comprehensive anti-bullying program is the most effective approach. This approach involves multiple stakeholders and promotes a holistic and preventive strategy. Options A, C, and D are not recommended and do not address the issue comprehensively.

QUESTION 125

Answer: C

Explanation: To promote participation and long-term engagement in a physical activity program, it is crucial to provide a variety of enjoyable physical activities that cater to diverse interests and abilities. Forcing participation, focusing solely on competition, or eliminating physical education classes may lead to resistance and disengagement.

QUESTION 126

Answer: B

Explanation: Collaborating with teachers, counselors, and families to identify and address the causes of absenteeism is a proactive and effective approach. It helps understand the underlying issues and implement targeted interventions. Options A, C, and D do not address the root causes and may exacerbate the problem.

QUESTION 127

Answer: B

Explanation: ESEA, currently known as the Every Student Succeeds Act (ESSA), focuses on improving educational outcomes for all students, including those with disabilities. It includes provisions related to accountability, assessment, and support services.

QUESTION 128

Answer: C

Explanation: ADA applies in a university setting to protect the rights of students with disabilities and ensure they receive reasonable accommodations to access educational opportunities.

QUESTION 129

Answer: A

Explanation: Section 504 of the Rehabilitation Act prohibits discrimination against individuals with disabilities in federally funded programs, including schools. It requires schools to provide reasonable accommodations to ensure equal access to educational services.

QUESTION 130

Answer: B

Explanation: It's important to consider that there might be various factors contributing to the difficulties both Sarah and Jake are experiencing. A comprehensive assessment can help pinpoint the underlying issues and guide appropriate interventions.

QUESTION 131

Answer: B

Explanation: Recognizing and nurturing Michael's exceptional talent in mathematics is crucial for his overall development. Providing advanced coursework or extracurricular activities allows him to thrive in his area of strength.

QUESTION 132

Answer: B

Explanation: Creating a positive reading environment at home, where reading is seen as an enjoyable activity, can significantly support Emily's progress. It encourages a love for reading, which is crucial for long-term success.

QUESTION 133

Answer: B

Explanation: Before implementing interventions, it is crucial to understand the function of Alex's aggressive behavior. A Functional Behavior Assessment (FBA) provides insights into the triggers and reinforces effective strategies for intervention.

QUESTION 134

Answer: C

Explanation: Engaging in group activities or clubs allows Lily to practice social skills in a natural setting while pursuing her interests. It provides opportunities for meaningful social interactions.

QUESTION 135

Answer: A

Explanation: A daily report card system provides immediate feedback and reinforcement for desired behaviors, helping to address Ryan's impulsive behavior in a structured and consistent manner.

QUESTION 136

Answer: B

Explanation: Based on Max's specific needs, targeted support in written expression is crucial. Offering structured writing activities and explicit instruction will help him develop this skill.

QUESTION 137

Answer: C

Explanation: A social skills curriculum within the classroom environment will provide Mia with structured opportunities to practice and improve her social interactions with peers.

QUESTION 138

Answer: B

Explanation: For Sarah, applying mathematical concepts to real-world situations can help bridge the gap between understanding and practical application, addressing her specific learning disability.

QUESTION 139

Answer: B

Explanation: For Jake, providing a structured note-taking system and breaks for movement during lectures will help him stay engaged and focused, allowing him to excel in mathematics.

QUESTION 140

Answer: C

Explanation: Addressing Emily's specific learning disability in reading comprehension through targeted strategies within the classroom setting will provide her with ongoing support in her areas of need.

QUESTION 141

Answer: A

Explanation: Providing Liam with a visual schedule will help him anticipate and prepare for transitions, reducing anxiety and supporting his engagement in classroom activities.

QUESTION 142

Answer: A

Explanation: It is crucial that the chosen assessment tool aligns with the school's curriculum and learning objectives to accurately measure the students' progress in their specific educational context.

QUESTION 143

Answer: A

Explanation: To ensure fair and accurate assessment for linguistically diverse students, it is essential that the assessment tool's norming sample includes a diverse range of linguistic backgrounds.

QUESTION 144

Answer: A

Explanation: Reviewing the previous evaluation results is crucial to identify any changes in Alex's academic performance since the initial evaluation. This will help in determining if reevaluation is warranted and in understanding the trajectory of his academic progress.

QUESTION 145

Answer: A

Explanation: Having the assessment available in the students' native languages ensures that the assessment accurately measures their reading proficiency, rather than their proficiency in English.

QUESTION 146

Answer: A

Explanation: It is important to conduct a thorough review of the intervention strategies to understand what has worked and what needs adjustment. This ensures that the interventions are tailored to the specific needs of each student.

QUESTION 147

Answer: A

Explanation: Ensuring that the assessment tool is culturally sensitive and appropriate for the diverse student population is essential for fair and accurate evaluation of all students, regardless of their cultural backgrounds.

QUESTION 148

Answer: A

Explanation: Given the significant discrepancy between Emily's verbal and nonverbal scores, it is important to explore potential language-related factors that may have influenced her verbal score. This investigation will provide a more comprehensive understanding of her cognitive abilities.

QUESTION 149

Answer: A

Explanation: The assessment results indicate a specific area of weakness (decoding) and a specific area of strength (reading comprehension). This suggests that targeted interventions should be implemented to address James' decoding skills.

QUESTION 150

Answer: A

Explanation: Alex's scores indicate a significant area of need in self-regulation. Therefore, the most appropriate recommendation is to focus on interventions targeting this specific area.

QUESTION 151

Answer: A

Explanation: The assessment findings provide valuable insights into the factors influencing Sarah's behavior. Developing a behavior intervention plan (BIP) based on this information will provide targeted support to address her specific needs.

QUESTION 152

Answer: A

Explanation: The assessment results highlight a specific area of need (fine motor skills). Therefore, the most appropriate recommendation is to implement targeted interventions to support Liam's development in this area.

QUESTION 153

Answer: B

Explanation: It is important to provide clear and accurate information about Jake's performance, particularly in mathematics, and to discuss appropriate interventions and support to address his specific needs in this area. This ensures that everyone involved is aware of the necessary steps to support Jake's academic progress.

QUESTION 154

Answer: B

Explanation: Classroom modifications can help create a more comfortable learning environment for Sarah, reducing anxiety triggers during math class.

QUESTION 155

Answer: A

Explanation: Individual counseling can help Jake understand and manage the underlying causes of his anger, which is a crucial step in addressing his behavior.

QUESTION 156

Answer: C

Explanation: Encouraging parental involvement in reading and homework support is an effective prevention and intervention strategy to enhance Mia's literacy skills and overall academic progress.

QUESTION 157

Answer: A

Explanation: Addressing Alex's substance abuse and depression through individual counseling is essential to provide him with the necessary support and intervention.

QUESTION 158

Answer: C

Explanation: Individual counseling can help Emily address her self-esteem issues and emotional well-being, providing her with essential support in her specific situation.

QUESTION 159

Answer: D

Explanation: Individual counseling can help identify the underlying causes of Liam's behavior, which is a crucial step in developing effective prevention and intervention strategies tailored to his specific needs.

QUESTION 160

Answer: C

Explanation: Individual counseling allows for a tailored approach to address Mark's specific grief reactions and provides a safe space for him to explore coping strategies.

QUESTION 161

Answer: C

Explanation: Individual counseling allows for a thorough assessment of Lily's specific anxiety triggers and the development of personalized strategies to address her test anxiety effectively.

QUESTION 162

Answer: A

Explanation: Critical Incident Stress Debriefing (CISD) sessions are designed to provide support and help individuals process the emotional impact of a crisis situation, making it the most appropriate model for this scenario.

QUESTION 163

Answer: C

Explanation: Individual counseling sessions can help uncover the underlying causes of Ethan's aggression and provide targeted strategies for behavior change.

QUESTION 164

Answer: A

Explanation: Collaborating with school personnel and community service providers through regular meetings is essential for coordinating efforts and ensuring a comprehensive and effective response to the crisis situation.

QUESTION 165

Answer: C

Explanation: Individual counseling sessions provide a safe and supportive space for Olivia to address her emotional distress and develop coping strategies to manage the effects of bullying.

QUESTION 166

Answer: A

Explanation: Actively listening, validating feelings, and providing support are essential for establishing trust and effective communication with parents who are expressing concerns.

QUESTION 167

Answer: A

Explanation: For a student like Jack who struggles with verbal expression of emotions, visual communication tools can provide a structured and effective way for him to communicate his feelings.

QUESTION 168

Answer: A

Explanation: Using visual aids and written instructions alongside verbal communication helps provide clear and accessible information for diverse learners, including ELLs and students with speech and language disabilities.

QUESTION 169

Answer: A

Explanation: Facilitating an IEP meeting involves active listening to various stakeholders, articulating ideas clearly, and guiding the discussion to ensure all relevant information is addressed effectively.

QUESTION 170

Answer: A

Explanation: For a student like Emily who benefits from visual supports, using visual schedules, charts, and diagrams alongside verbal instructions can enhance her understanding and comprehension.

QUESTION 171

Answer: A

Explanation: Providing translated written materials and offering interpreters ensures that parents from diverse cultural backgrounds with varying English proficiency levels can access and understand important information effectively.

QUESTION 172

Answer: B

Explanation: As a school psychologist, your initial role in this situation is to serve as a case manager for the assessment process. This involves coordinating with relevant stakeholders, gathering information, and overseeing the evaluation process.

QUESTION 173

Answer: A

Explanation: One of the key responsibilities of the school psychologist in a multidisciplinary team meeting is to provide recommendations for instructional strategies and accommodations that will support the student's needs as outlined in the IEP.

QUESTION 174

Answer: A

Explanation: Gathering baseline data before implementing the intervention is crucial for evaluating its effectiveness. This data serves as a point of comparison to measure any improvements in the students' reading abilities.

QUESTION 175

Answer: A

Explanation: Conducting observations in various settings and situations is a critical step in a functional-behavioral assessment. This helps identify triggers, patterns, and potential interventions to address Sarah's behavioral difficulties.

QUESTION 176

Answer: A

Explanation: When assisting school administrators in problem-solving and decision-making, it is crucial to collaborate with them and gather relevant data and information to ensure a comprehensive and informed approach.

QUESTION 177

Answer: A

Explanation: As the case manager for a reevaluation, a key responsibility is to coordinate with relevant stakeholders to gather updated assessment data and input. This ensures that the reevaluation is comprehensive and informed.

QUESTION 178

Answer: A

Explanation: State policies and procedures typically require a comprehensive evaluation to determine eligibility for special education services. This evaluation helps ensure that students receive appropriate support based on their individual needs.

QUESTION 179

Answer: A

Explanation: One of the key responsibilities of the school psychologist is to collaborate with the IEP team to develop and implement an appropriate IEP that addresses Emily's specific needs.

QUESTION 180

Answer: A

Explanation: State policies require that students' rights to due process and procedural safeguards are upheld during the disciplinary process. This ensures fairness and protection of the student's rights.

QUESTION 181

Answer: A

Explanation: Recognizing and respecting cultural differences is an important consideration when applying state policies to ensure equity. This helps address the unique needs of students and their families.

QUESTION 182

Answer: A

Explanation: State policies require a review of a student's educational records and, if necessary, assessments to determine appropriate placement and services when transitioning to a new school district.

QUESTION 183

Answer: A

Explanation: One of the key responsibilities of the school psychologist in the committee is to advocate for equitable graduation requirements that consider the diverse needs of all students, ensuring that they have the opportunity to succeed and graduate.

QUESTION 184

Answer: B

Explanation: Journaling can help the student develop self-awareness by reflecting on their emotions and understanding the triggers for their tantrums. This promotes emotional development by allowing the student to identify and manage their feelings effectively.

QUESTION 185

Answer: B

Explanation: Open-ended, imaginative play stimulates creativity, problem-solving, and cognitive development in preschool children. It allows them to explore their interests and develop critical thinking skills, making it an effective strategy for promoting cognitive development.

QUESTION 186

Answer: B

Explanation: Providing praise and constructive feedback can boost the student's self-esteem and motivation, leading to improved academic performance. It also supports emotional development by fostering a positive self-image and confidence.

QUESTION 187

Answer: C

Explanation: Regular conversation and reading activities provide opportunities for language stimulation and development. Engaging in meaningful verbal interactions with the child is essential for improving their language and communication skills, making option C the correct choice.

QUESTION 188

Answer: C

Explanation: Interactive e-books combine technology with reading, offering engaging multimedia elements and interactive features that can improve reading comprehension. This approach aligns with the student's interest in technology while addressing their reading difficulties.

QUESTION 189

Answer: B

Explanation: Social skills training can help the student improve their ability to interact effectively with peers and navigate various school settings. While math skills are important, addressing social difficulties is crucial for overall effective functioning in school.

QUESTION 190

Answer: C

Explanation: Incorporating interactive and hands-on activities can engage the student's attention and facilitate their learning. This modification aligns with the student's need for a more dynamic learning environment and enhances their learning opportunities.

QUESTION 191

Answer: B

Explanation: Individualizing curriculum and instruction is essential to address the diverse learning needs of students effectively. This approach promotes tailored learning experiences and better supports student success, aligning with the topic's focus on appropriate recommendations for curriculum and instructional modifications.

QUESTION 192

Answer: A

Explanation: A traditional standardized language assessment provides structured, norm-referenced data on a child's language development, making it a suitable choice for addressing concerns in this context. While observation and parent interviews can complement the assessment, they alone may not provide the necessary data for informed decisions.

QUESTION 193

Answer: B

Explanation: Administering a comprehensive math achievement battery provides detailed information about the student's math skills and weaknesses, enabling the development of targeted interventions. This assessment directly informs intervention planning and decision-making.

QUESTION 194

Answer: C

Explanation: A scaffolded reading comprehension assessment provides support and guidance to students during the assessment, allowing you to observe their potential for improvement and their specific areas of difficulty. This directly informs intervention strategies tailored to their needs.

QUESTION 195

Answer: C

Explanation: A functional behavior assessment systematically analyzes the function or purpose of the student's challenging behaviors. This assessment provides critical insights into the causes of the behaviors and guides the development of appropriate interventions and educational placements.

QUESTION 196

Answer: D

Explanation: A standardized articulation test assesses specific speech and language skills and provides norm-referenced data, making it valuable for addressing concerns about speech and language delays in preschool children. While observations and parent interviews are useful, they may not offer the specificity needed for appropriate recommendations.

QUESTION 197

Answer: B

Explanation: To determine the presence and nature of giftedness in a student from a culturally diverse background, a comprehensive assessment that considers multiple domains and is culturally sensitive is essential. Relying solely on one domain or standardized scores may not accurately identify giftedness in all areas.

QUESTION 198

Answer: B

Explanation: While standardized test scores can be an indicator, assessing giftedness should also consider factors like motivation and creativity, which may not be fully captured by standardized assessments. These factors can provide valuable insights into the nature of the student's giftedness.

QUESTION 199

Answer: B

Explanation: Using culturally fair and unbiased assessment tools and procedures is essential to ensure that all students, regardless of their cultural background, have an equal opportunity to be identified as gifted. This aligns with principles of fairness and equity in education.

QUESTION 200

Answer: B

Explanation: Prioritizing a culturally sensitive assessment of the student's exceptional mathematical abilities allows for a more accurate evaluation of their giftedness while considering their cultural and linguistic background. This approach is more likely to identify their unique strengths.

QUESTION 201

Answer: B

Explanation: In this scenario, addressing the student's social and emotional challenges within the general education classroom is a reasonable initial step. It allows the student to remain in the general education setting while receiving targeted support for their emotional needs. Placing them in a self-contained gifted classroom might not address their social and emotional struggles effectively.

QUESTION 202

Answer: A

Explanation: Placing the student in a general education classroom with speech therapy allows them to benefit from the general education curriculum while receiving targeted support for their speech and language disorder. This inclusionary approach promotes social interaction with peers and maximizes learning opportunities.

QUESTION 203

Answer: B

Explanation: When a student continues to struggle despite RTI interventions, it is appropriate to consider an IEP that provides more specialized and individualized support. In this case, specialized reading instruction tailored to the student's needs can address their learning disability effectively.

QUESTION 204

Answer: A

Explanation: Developing an IHCP allows the student to receive necessary medical care while remaining in the general education classroom. This option promotes inclusion and ensures the student can access the curriculum while addressing their health needs.

QUESTION 205

Answer: A

Explanation: Placing the student in an ESL program with additional math support recognizes the importance of addressing their language needs while also providing enrichment in mathematics. This approach ensures that the student's unique combination of needs is addressed effectively.

QUESTION 206

Answer: C

Explanation: Given the student's financial limitations, connecting them with a community-based mental health clinic that offers sliding-scale fees ensures they can receive psychological support without a significant financial burden. This option considers both the student's needs and their financial situation.

QUESTION 207

Answer: B

Explanation: A school-based behavior intervention plan is designed to address behavioral issues within the educational setting. It focuses on targeted interventions and support strategies to improve behavior and foster a positive learning environment.

QUESTION 208

Answer: D

Explanation: The RTI program is a school-based resource that provides targeted academic support to students who are struggling. It is a recommended first step in addressing academic difficulties within the school system, and it can help identify and support students with learning disabilities.

QUESTION 209

Answer: D

Explanation: Community-based support groups for teens dealing with substance abuse provide a supportive and understanding environment for addressing this issue. They often involve peers who have experienced similar challenges and can be a valuable resource for the student's recovery.

QUESTION 210

Answer: D

Explanation: The IHCP team at the school can collaborate with the student's healthcare providers to develop a plan that addresses the student's health needs while ensuring they receive appropriate educational services. This approach maintains the connection to the school environment and supports the student's education during health-related absences.

QUESTION 211

Answer: C

Explanation: To promote change effectively, it's important to provide comprehensive training that not only covers the technical aspects of the new technology but also demonstrates its practical use in the educational context. This approach ensures that staff can effectively utilize the system to benefit students.

QUESTION 212

Answer: C

Explanation: Effective consultation and collaboration at the district level require open and transparent communication among team members with diverse expertise. This approach promotes a shared understanding of the issues and potential solutions, leading to meaningful change.

QUESTION 213

Answer: C

Explanation: Clear communication with a diverse audience, such as parents, requires active listening to their concerns and using plain language to convey complex concepts. It is important to address their specific concerns and ensure that information is easily understood to foster collaboration and understanding.

QUESTION 214

Answer: C

Explanation: To promote change at the classroom level, it is essential to collaborate with teachers and involve them in the decision-making process. Understanding their concerns and needs allows for the development of effective strategies that are more likely to be embraced and implemented successfully.

QUESTION 215

Answer: C

Explanation: In a situation with differing opinions, facilitating open and constructive dialogue among stakeholders, including administrators, policy makers, teachers, and students, is crucial. This approach allows for a comprehensive exploration of the issues and potential solutions, leading to more effective decision-making.

QUESTION 216

Answer: B

Explanation: To design an effective and fair discipline policy, it is crucial to base it on research-backed practices that promote positive behavior and minimize negative outcomes. Conducting a comprehensive review of research allows for an evidence-based approach that considers the best interests of students.

QUESTION 217

Answer: C

Explanation: Effective staff development should be individualized and tailored to address the specific needs and roles of different staff members within the school system. This approach ensures that professional development is relevant and impactful.

QUESTION 218

Answer: C

Explanation: Grading policies should strike a balance between consistency and flexibility to address the diverse needs of students. Effective grading policies consider both standardized criteria and individual student circumstances.

QUESTION 219

Answer: C

Explanation: Promoting inclusive practices that integrate students with disabilities into general education settings is a fundamental aspect of effective special education programs. Inclusion benefits both students with disabilities and their peers, fostering a more inclusive and supportive learning environment.

QUESTION 220

Answer: C

Explanation: To support ELL students effectively, staff development initiatives should incorporate strategies that address their unique needs, including language proficiency and cultural sensitivity. Ignoring these factors can hinder the success of ELL students in the classroom.

QUESTION 221

Answer: B

Explanation: To make informed decisions about the effectiveness of an intervention program, it is essential to use multiple data sources and measures, including qualitative and quantitative data. Relying solely on one type of data may not provide a comprehensive picture of program success.

QUESTION 222

Answer: B

Explanation: Effective data-based decision making involves ongoing monitoring and evaluation of programs to assess their long-term impact and address concerns that may arise. Relying solely on short-term data may not provide a comprehensive understanding of a program's effectiveness.

QUESTION 223

Answer: B

Explanation: Surveys can provide in-depth insights by gathering perspectives and opinions from teachers and parents, who may have valuable information about the factors contributing to student absenteeism. This method allows for a more comprehensive understanding of the issue.

QUESTION 224

Answer: C

Explanation: Effective data-based decision making involves tailoring professional development strategies to address specific student performance data and the unique needs of teachers and students. This approach ensures that professional development is targeted and relevant.

QUESTION 225

Answer: C

Explanation: Ethical data-based decision making requires safeguarding the privacy and confidentiality of student and staff information. This ensures that sensitive data are protected and used responsibly in program evaluations, respecting the rights and privacy of individuals.

QUESTION 226

Answer: A

Explanation: Option A is the correct answer because it involves a proactive approach to address Alex's behavior. By implementing a behavior modification plan with both rewards and consequences, you are reinforcing positive behavior and discouraging disruptive behavior through a systematic and evidence-based approach. Options B, C, and D do not address the underlying causes of the behavior or provide a structured intervention plan.

QUESTION 227

Answer: B

Explanation: Option B is the correct answer because it focuses on a proactive approach to address bullying behavior. Developing a comprehensive anti-bullying program is essential in creating a safe and supportive school environment. Options A, C, and D do not provide effective strategies for addressing the root causes of bullying or preventing it from occurring.

QUESTION 228

Answer: B

Explanation: Option B is the correct answer because it provides a structured intervention approach that addresses the group's specific needs. Group therapy sessions can help students learn social skills, practice them with peers, and receive feedback in a supportive environment. Options A, C, and D do not offer effective strategies for addressing the social skills deficits of the group.

QUESTION 229

Answer: B

Explanation: Option B is the correct answer because it offers a constructive and evidence-based approach to help Sarah manage her anxiety. Relaxation and mindfulness techniques can be effective in reducing anxiety symptoms and improving concentration. Options A, C, and D are not appropriate and may exacerbate Sarah's anxiety.

QUESTION 230

Answer: D

Explanation: Option D is the correct answer because it addresses the specific area of concern, which is Emily's number sense. Standardized achievement tests (Option A) may not provide detailed information on specific deficits, and a comprehensive neuropsychological assessment (Option B) may be too extensive for addressing this specific issue. Curriculum-based assessments (Option C) may not isolate and assess the specific number sense deficit.

QUESTION 231

Answer: B

Explanation: Option B is the correct answer because it allows for a detailed examination of Daniel's specific reading difficulties, helping to pinpoint areas in need of intervention. Group-administered tests (Option A) may not provide the necessary level of detail, and general intelligence tests (Option C) do not focus specifically on reading. Teacher observations (Option D) can be valuable but should be complemented with formal assessments for a comprehensive understanding of Daniel's reading skills.

QUESTION 232

Answer: C

Explanation: Option C is the correct answer because it allows for a comprehensive evaluation of Alex's language proficiency in both languages, recognizing his diverse linguistic background. Options A and B focus solely on English proficiency, which may not provide a complete picture, and Option D lacks the structured assessment needed for accurate evaluation.

QUESTION 233

Answer: D

Explanation: Option D is the correct answer because it aligns with Maria's specific needs as a student with a visual impairment. It ensures that the assessment is accessible and adapted to her condition. Options A, B, and C do not address the unique challenges posed by Maria's visual impairment and may not provide accurate information about her reading abilities.

QUESTION 234

Answer: C

Explanation: Option C is the correct answer because it recognizes the importance of addressing both academic and emotional needs in a holistic manner. By integrating support, the team can provide comprehensive interventions that respond to James's identified needs. Options A, B, and D focus on only one aspect of James's needs and do not address the multidisciplinary approach.

QUESTION 235

Answer: C

Explanation: Option C is the correct answer because it recognizes the importance of conducting a comprehensive assessment to understand the root causes of Sarah's attention difficulties before implementing any interventions. Options A and D jump to interventions without sufficient assessment, and Option B focuses solely on academic accommodations without addressing the underlying issues.

QUESTION 236

Answer: C

Explanation: Option C is the correct answer because systematic desensitization is an evidence-based approach to reducing test anxiety by gradually exposing the student to anxiety-provoking situations. Options A, B, and D do not address the underlying anxiety issue or provide a comprehensive intervention strategy.

QUESTION 237

Answer: B

Explanation: Option B is the correct answer because it addresses the specific deficit identified through assessment (phonemic awareness) and provides targeted intervention to strengthen Mia's foundational reading skills. Options A, C, and D do not directly address the identified issue and may not be as effective in improving Mia's reading comprehension.

QUESTION 238

Answer: C

Explanation: This option recognizes the interrelationship between Sarah's difficulties in reading and social interactions, suggesting that there may be an underlying developmental issue affecting both domains. It highlights the importance of considering multiple domains when assessing a student's challenges.

QUESTION 239

Answer: C

Explanation: This option recognizes the mutual influence between cognitive and language development, highlighting that each domain supports and enhances the other. It reflects an understanding of the interconnected nature of these developmental domains.

QUESTION 240

Answer: C

Explanation: This option acknowledges that Jake's advanced cognitive abilities may contribute to his frustration when interacting with peers who may not meet his intellectual expectations. It demonstrates an understanding of the potential interplay between cognitive and social/emotional development.

QUESTION 241

Answer: A

Explanation: This option demonstrates the interrelationship between improved social skills and enhanced cognitive performance. Emma's better classroom behavior and focus during math lessons can be attributed to her improved social/emotional development, highlighting the impact of one domain on the other.

QUESTION 242

Answer: A

Explanation: Sarah's struggles with learning are most likely influenced by biological factors related to her brain development, which can impact her cognitive abilities and academic performance. While other factors like socioeconomic status, teacher expectations, and cultural background can also play a role, the question asks for the factor most likely contributing to her difficulties.

QUESTION 243

Answer: B

Explanation: This option recognizes that psychopathological factors can have a significant impact on both emotional and cognitive functioning, which can impair both social and academic development. It demonstrates an understanding of the broad-reaching effects of psychopathological factors on students' learning.

QUESTION 244

Answer: A

Explanation: David's impulsive behavior in the classroom is most likely influenced by biological factors related to his temperament, which can affect his self-control and ability to regulate his impulses. While other factors like cultural background, family issues, and teacher expectations can also play a role, the question asks for the factor most likely contributing to his behavior.

QUESTION 245

Answer: B

Explanation: This option recognizes that family issues can influence a student's learning by affecting their motivation and home environment, which can, in turn, impact their academic performance. It reflects an understanding of the complex interplay between family issues and students' learning.

QUESTION 246

Answer: C

Explanation: Maria's lack of interest in math and her struggles with completing assignments are indicative of issues with student motivation, which is most likely contributing to her difficulties in the subject. While other factors like socioeconomic status, parent expectations, and prenatal and early environment can also play a role, the question asks for the factor most likely contributing to her math difficulties.

QUESTION 247

Answer: B

Explanation: A structured observation of Sarah's reading behavior allows for a non-threatening and natural assessment of her reading difficulties in the classroom environment. Standardized tests and quizzes may induce anxiety in some students, while a teacher interview may not provide direct, observable data on Sarah's reading behavior.

QUESTION 248

Answer: C

Explanation: Curriculum-based assessments (CBAs) are designed to offer frequent and direct assessments of students' academic skills within their classroom context. They help educators track students' progress in the curriculum and identify areas where additional support may be needed.

QUESTION 249

Answer: C

Explanation: A behavioral checklist completed by the teacher is the most appropriate assessment instrument for evaluating James's social and emotional development in a classroom setting. It provides specific observations and insights into his behavior and social interactions. IQ tests and standardized achievement tests are not designed for assessing social and emotional development, and a parent interview may not capture classroom behaviors adequately.

QUESTION 250

Answer: C

Explanation: When selecting an assessment instrument for evaluating a student with a suspected learning disability, the school psychologist should consider the validity and reliability of the instrument for the specific student population. This ensures that the assessment accurately measures the student's abilities and provides reliable results. Factors like popularity, cost, and online resources are secondary to the instrument's appropriateness for the given context.

QUESTION 251

Answer: C

Explanation: A speech and language assessment conducted by a speech therapist is the most appropriate assessment instrument for evaluating Emily's language development and potential speech delays. It involves specialized tools and expertise to assess language skills accurately. Standardized intelligence tests and multiple-choice vocabulary tests are not designed for this purpose, and a parent interview may not provide the necessary clinical assessment.

QUESTION 252

Answer: B

Explanation: When assessing a student with a visual impairment like Julia, it is essential to adapt the assessment by providing it in braille or using appropriate assistive technology to ensure she can access and respond to the assessment content effectively. While lighting conditions, additional time, and sensory breaks may be necessary for some students, the primary adaptation for Julia should address her visual impairment.

QUESTION 253

Answer: C

Explanation: Procedural modifications can make assessments more accessible for students with special needs without necessarily affecting the validity of the results. When done appropriately, these modifications ensure that the assessment accurately measures the intended construct while accommodating the individual needs of the student.

QUESTION 254

Answer: A

Explanation: Providing extra time for completing the assessment is a common procedural modification for students with ADHD, as it allows them to work at their own pace and minimizes the impact of impulsivity and distractibility. While breaks and shorter assessments may be appropriate for some students, extra time is a specific accommodation for ADHD.

QUESTION 255

Answer: C

Explanation: Making modifications to the assessment to accommodate the student's individual needs is essential to ensure the assessment's validity when assessing a student who requires special education services. This ensures that the assessment accurately measures the student's abilities while addressing any barriers they may face. While minimizing distractions and following standardized procedures are important, they may not be sufficient for students with special needs.

QUESTION 256

Answer: B

Explanation: Administering the assessment orally can be a valuable procedural modification for a student with dyslexia, as it allows them to demonstrate their reading abilities without being hindered by their reading difficulties. While other modifications like larger font size, reducing the number of items, and extending time limits may be appropriate for some students, an oral assessment directly addresses Michael's needs related to dyslexia.

QUESTION 257

Answer: B

Explanation: To ensure a fair and accurate cognitive assessment for Emily, it is essential to translate the assessment into her native language to ensure she fully comprehends the content. This accommodation aligns with best practices for assessing ELL students, as it minimizes language barriers and provides a more accurate representation of her cognitive abilities. Administering the assessment solely in English may not effectively assess Emily's true cognitive potential, and visual aids alone may not be sufficient to address language-related challenges. Extending the time limit (option C) is not as effective as providing the assessment in her native language.

QUESTION 258

Answer: B

Explanation: To accommodate Daniel's needs due to ADHD, it is essential to allow him to take breaks during the assessment when needed. This accommodation aligns with best practices for students with ADHD, as it helps him manage impulsivity and attention difficulties. Administering the assessment in a quiet room (option A) is a good practice but may not be sufficient for addressing ADHD-related challenges. Using a smaller font size (option C) or a shorter assessment (option D) does not directly address ADHD-related difficulties.

QUESTION 259

Answer: A

Explanation: To ensure an accurate evaluation of Sarah's reading abilities, it is appropriate to provide her with additional time to complete the assessment. This accommodation allows Sarah to demonstrate her reading skills without the time pressure that exacerbates her difficulties. Using a different assessment (option B) that does not involve reading may not accurately assess her reading abilities. Assessing her without accommodations (option C) would not consider her documented learning disability. Providing a peer reader (option D) may not be an appropriate accommodation for a standardized reading assessment.